The World Comes to America

The World Comes to America

Immigration to the United States Since 1945

LEONARD DINNERSTEIN
University of Arizona

DAVID M. REIMERS
New York University

New York   Oxford
OXFORD UNIVERSITY PRESS

Oxford University Press is a department of the University of Oxford. It furthers the University's
objective of excellence in research, scholarship, and education.

Oxford   New York
Auckland   Cape Town   Dar es Salaam   Hong Kong   Karachi
Kuala Lumpur   Madrid   Melbourne   Mexico City   Nairobi
New Delhi   Shanghai   Taipei   Toronto

With offices in
Argentina   Austria   Brazil   Chile   Czech Republic   France   Greece
Guatemala   Hungary   Italy   Japan   Poland   Portugal   Singapore
South Korea   Switzerland   Thailand   Turkey   Ukraine   Vietnam

Copyright © 2014 by Oxford University Press.

For titles covered by Section 112 of the US Higher Education Opportunity
Act, please visit www.oup.com/us/he for the latest information about
pricing and alternate formats.

Published by Oxford University Press.
198 Madison Avenue, New York, New York 10016
http://www.oup.com

Oxford is a registered trademark of Oxford University Press

ISBN 978-0-19-538478-9

To Corky and Myra

CONTENTS

PREFACE

The World Comes to America is a comprehensive survey of the people who arrived in the United States since 1945 and the immigration policy changes that facilitated this movement. Too often general accounts of American history, including those dealing with the post-1945 era, neglect these changes. Large numbers have arrived since the 1960s; over twenty million immigrants alone entered from 1990 to 2010, the most in any twenty-year period in American history. This immigration is changing American society, and will continue to do so for the foreseeable future.

We write about who came, why they came, where they went, and how they engaged with American culture and the economy. American policies changed significantly with the passage of the Immigration Act of 1965 and subsequent laws and led to a major transformation in the national origins of immigrants to the United States. In 1945 about 90 percent of Americans traced their ancestry to Europe. Today Europeans represent only two-thirds of the American population; immigration accounts for this change. Most immigrants in the past sixty-five years, and especially since the 1980s, hail from Latin America, Asia, the Middle East, and Africa.

We believe that the sources of immigrants to the United States shifted because American policies and attitudes about whom would be welcomed changed. Before World War II most Americans were descendants of English, German, and Irish immigrants, who favored newcomers from countries in Western Europe. We believe that after 1945 shifts occurred partly because of growing ethnic toleration in American society. We are aware, of course, that Americans have always been ambivalent about newcomers and often talk of building walls and excluding some groups, but nonetheless the decline of ethnic prejudice has been significant. Also important is the emergence of the United States as the world's leading power, which required significant changes in foreign, military, and to some extent, domestic policies. The American government committed itself to a major involvement in world affairs, and American culture expanded throughout the world. Moreover, as a result of a new US presence in other nations, different peoples learned about the opportunities in the United States and absorbed aspects of American culture from the men and women who brought it to their countries.

Although the origins of most immigrants to the United States in recent decades differ from most of those who came before them, they, like the newcomers of yesteryear, contribute to the growth and strength of the nation. Moreover, their various cultural values enrich and enliven an already sparkling array of different local, regional, and national attributes. As always occurred in the past, the changing nature of the sources of immigrants present some challenges before the foreigners and their offspring blend into and are comfortable with other Americans, but we also argue that their presence confirms beliefs that the United States is still a land of opportunity for enterprising individuals from every part of the globe.

Historians are often indebted to the works and assistance of others. Friends and scholars, Fred Binder, Fred Jaher, and George Lankevich read chapter drafts and offered valuable suggestions for improvement. We also appreciate the work of Kat Morgan, who supplied many of the tables, graphs, and charts; and that of Rebecca Reimers, who helped copyedit the manuscript.

Many of Oxford University Press's readers made detailed suggestions for our consideration as we rewrote the manuscript. We thank them for their efforts: Brian D. Behnken, Iowa State University; Barbara Blumberg, Pace University; Sylvie Coulibaly, Kenyon College; John Enyeart, Bucknell University; and Andrew E. Kersten, University of Wisconsin, Green Bay. Above all, our editor, Brian Wheel, provided insightful comments. Any misstatements as well as errors of fact or interpretation are our own.

Leonard Dinnerstein
David M. Reimers
August 15, 2012

INTRODUCTION

The goal of this book is to present a brief overview of the groups of immigrants who arrived in the United States after World War II ended in 1945. We indicate who came, explain their reasons for immigrating, note where they settled, and to a limited extent discuss how they fared once they arrived. In pursuing these goals we discuss conflicting American attitudes toward welcoming strangers and the different policies that Congress pursued either to aid or retard the entry of foreigners to America.

Migration is, and frequently has been, a global phenomenon, and people have moved to and from every continent in the world. Most of those who sought and achieved new lives in the United States and elsewhere did so to obtain greater economic opportunities for themselves and their families. A variety of other, but subsidiary, factors often converged to motivate people to pick themselves up and seek their fortunes elsewhere. Among immigration historians, the term used for these motivators is "push-pull" factors. That is, what the causes were that stimulated the exodus (push factors) and what the attractions were in the new locations (pull factors) that influenced individual decisions. Among the "push" factors were wars, revolutions, and fears of persecution. Among the "pull" factors, aside from economics, were greater political freedom, family unification, and educational opportunities. Of course, in some circumstances, what we label as "subsidiary" motivating factors were, in fact, the major or only reasons for movement. One might list among these other causes the Holocaust in World War II Europe; the communist takeover of several nations in Eastern Europe, China, and Latin America; and the dismantling of the European colonial system in Africa and Asia after 1945. Moreover the influence of military occupations in different nations, the growth of technology, and the spread of knowledge about different cultures cannot be ignored. Finally, the greater ease of movement allowed by new and faster means of transportation facilitated the migrations of peoples from one location to another.

While acknowledging the various global movements and experiences, we must again emphasize that this work is a brief overview of the factors that led to increased immigration to the United States since the end of World War II. In this overview, we occasionally highlight other world events while presenting the realities of worldwide migration.

Immigration is the lifeblood of America. Since the colonial era millions of foreigners have come to America seeking greater economic opportunities and a more stable lifestyle. The British settled in what is now the East Coast of the United States and set up the institutions that have remained basic to society. In what are now the southwestern and western parts of the country, Hispanics coming through Mexico planted the seeds of their European heritage. Several generations of intermarriage between them and the Indians already living there resulted in the development of a Mexican culture in many parts of the West.

The Netherlands, Great Britain, Ireland, Scotland, and the German states provided the largest numbers of newcomers to colonial America. Smatterings of other Europeans appeared, who blended in with the existing populations. Involuntary immigrants arrived from Africa, but they constituted a population of second-class citizens who were placed in slavery with little chance to obtain freedom. When the nation was established in the 1780s, the founding fathers patterned the government on institutions that then existed in England.

From the eighteenth through the twentieth-centuries western Europeans journeyed to the United States, with six million Germans and five million Irish topping the lists. In the middle of the nineteenth century the Chinese, along with South Americans and western Europeans, appeared in California seeking gold, and toward the end of the century the bulk of immigrants to the United States settled east of the Mississippi River, north of the Ohio River, and south of Canada. They included four million Italians, three million Slavs, and two million Jews overwhelming all others even though there were over one million Scandinavians, perhaps half a million Hungarians, and untold numbers of Filipinos and Japanese from Asia who remained mainly in California and other parts of the West.

The changing nature of the ethnic composition of immigrants alarmed people already in the United States who wanted to keep the nation white and Protestant. Americans preferred keeping non-Caucasians already in the United States in subservient positions. In the late nineteenth century Congress began passing legislation curbing untoward immigration. As a result, the Chinese Exclusion Act of 1882 suspended, and subsequently excluded most immigrants from China. Skillfully crafted legislation passed in the 1920s provided the largest quotas to natives of Great Britain, Germany, and Ireland while sharply curtailing the numbers of foreigners considered inferior to white, Anglo-Saxon, Protestants (WASPs). This led to drastic cuts in the numbers of Italians, Slavs, and Jews who might qualify for future admission. The law also eliminated the possibilities of practically any additional immigrants from Asia. Legislation favoring northern and western European immigrants remained in effect through 1968. Two Asian groups, however, received special consideration. In 1934 the United States declared its intention of allowing its colony in the Philippines to become independent and established a yearly quota for Filipinos of 50, which was to end a decade later; in 1943, as a wartime gesture to American allies in China, an act was passed to provide the Chinese with a quota of 105 persons per year. Then in 1946 the United States gave a quota to the Philippines of 100.

When the war ended in 1945, the United States assumed new responsibilities. Other countries looked to America, as the most powerful nation in the world, for guidance. Not only was the United States expected to lead in solving many of the world's problems but also American immigration policy could no longer be treated as an exclusively domestic concern. There were over a million refugees in central Europe, and our allies expected the United States to admit some and help relocate others. This expectation conflicted with the views of most Americans, who did not want to alter existing restrictions.

American intransigence and allies' petitions resulted in major foreign policy problems for President Harry S. Truman as he tried to lead Europeans in rebuilding torn societies while encouraging them to adopt cultural and democratic values similar to those that existed in the United States. People of other nations questioned the morality and humanity of Americans who refused to invite some of the displaced people to live in the United States, groups living under totalitarian systems, and individuals seeking opportunities to improve their lives elsewhere.

In 1945 the most publicized group of European homeless people was the Jews who had survived the Holocaust and who sought entry into the United States and/ or Palestine. American immigration laws limited their opportunities, as did British concerns in the Middle East, where the Arabs controlled vast oil deposits and a passageway to colonies in Asia. These problems were eventually sorted out, but not before some Americans reexamined what positions their government should assume in the post–World War II world.

In the following chapters we begin with the European displaced persons, Jews as well as gentiles, and their concerns in the mid-1940s. We then examine the different European groups whose fairly large quotas provided greater opportunities to emigrate to the United States. In the first chapter we also deal with the problems of war brides—spouses who married Americans during the war but who were not legally eligible to enter the United States with their husbands or wives—and Asians whose post–World War II goals changed as many of them sought entry to America. Essentially, the first chapter details the different groups that wanted to get to the United States and how Congress and the president dealt with them.

The Displaced Persons Acts of 1948 and 1950 made inroads toward solving the problem of homeless people in Europe, while the most controversial piece of legislation redefining American immigration policy, the McCarran-Walter Act, passed over President Truman's veto in 1952. This act repeated the national origin quotas established by the legislation of the 1920s but eliminated the ban on Asians entering the United States and gave every Asian nation a quota of one hundred.

Additional provisions of the bill barred communists from admission to the United States and stipulated special provisions to aid people escaping from communist countries. In the 1950s and 1960s both Hungarians and Cubans benefited from American concern about communist domination in their countries.

During the postwar decades many liberal Americans recognized that fairly rigid immigration laws not only hurt the image of the United States abroad but damaged its economy as well. Throughout American history immigrants fueled economic growth, but with strong barriers in place since the 1920s, groups of Americans worried that the economy might not thrive as it had in earlier centuries. Moreover, many Americans questioned the morality of choosing immigrants on the basis of race, religion, and/or political associations. Liberals triumphed in the election of 1964, and the presence of Lyndon B. Johnson in the White House resulted in strong presidential leadership and direction. In 1965 new legislation sponsored by the Democratic senator Philip Hart of Michigan, and the Democratic representative Emanuel Celler of New York, provided other methods for screening newcomers. The Immigration Act of 1965 eliminated all ethnic quotas in the Eastern Hemisphere and in their stead placed twenty-thousand-person caps on immigrants from each nation (not counting immediate family members of US citizens) and for the first time placed a ceiling on people emigrating from the Western Hemisphere. For the Eastern Hemisphere the new law favored unification of families in the United States with close relatives from abroad and also stipulated provisions that would bring people into the United States who could help propel the American economy. It also provided for the admission of 10,200 refugees. In 1978 Congress finally created a uniform system by combining the two hemispheres. The new world system provided for 290,000 immigrants, excluding immediate family members of US citizens.

Passage of the Immigration Act of 1965, while curtailing immigration from South America, and Central America, and North America, provided equality of opportunity for immigrants from the rest of the world. It also led to the most significant changes in American immigration policy since the restrictive acts of the 1920s, and paved the way, as well, for millions of Europeans, Asians, and Africans to enter the United States. There were other immigration regulatory changes after passage of the Immigration Act of 1965, but two were especially important. One, in 1986, opened the door for amnesty for millions who had entered the country illegally and another, in 1990, sought to bring in more Europeans, who had lost out by the changes made in the 1965 law. The 1990 legislation also provided more places for skilled immigrants. Some Americans, and hence their representatives, wanted more European immigrants because they were Caucasian and they believed that the potential for receiving more talented workers was greater if a larger number of Europeans reached American shores. As a result, not only did greater numbers of Irish and Polish people qualify for admission but also, after European communism collapsed in 1989, emigrants from Eastern Europe, heretofore barred by emigration restrictions, no longer had to contend with these barriers.

As a result of the 1986 law, over one million foreigners were admitted to the United States in 1989. It was the first time since 1914 that more than one million immigrants reached American shores in one year, and it marked the beginning of a two-decade flow of a massive number of people coming to the United States. In the 1990s over ten million immigrants arrived, the largest ten-year influx in American history, and in the first decade of the twenty-first century another ten million immigrants arrived. In addition, since the 1980s, over ten million undocumented immigrants also entered the country.

People arrived from every part of the world as the American economy expanded and workers filled jobs at various skill levels. Unskilled workers came mostly from Latin America, especially Mexico and Central America, while highly skilled people arrived not only from Latin America but also from Asia and Africa. Moreover, the 1990s witnessed a major change in the destination of millions of newer arrivals. For the first time in American history more foreigners went directly to suburbs and small towns throughout the nation. To be sure, major immigration destinations like the cities and surrounding areas of New York, Chicago, and Los Angeles continued to attract the largest number of newcomers, but the foreigners also found homes and established enclaves in the cities, and especially the suburbs, of places like Atlanta, Philadelphia, Minneapolis, Las Vegas, Houston, Seattle, and Dallas. The new immigrants' settlement patterns reflected the fact that economic opportunities existed in the suburbs of metropolitan areas, as well as in small towns in the South, the Midwest, and the West, where manufacturers had established plants that employed many of the least skilled foreigners.

The arrival of so many millions in the United States also spawned a great outcry from many Americans who believed that most immigrants were both Mexican and illegal. At the beginning of the twenty-first century over one-third of the newcomers, counting both legal and illegal, hailed from Mexico. Undocumented immigrants arrived from other nations as well, but lack of publicity about them resulted in their absence from American imagery. Their labor was needed, and whether they had proper documents was secondary. American agricultural enterprises, manufacturing firms, and service establishments did not care how the laborers arrived but they did know that they could pay them less than documented immigrants or Americans who had been born and educated in the country.

Today the United States has large communities of Mexicans, mostly in the southwest and in California, but scattered throughout the Midwest, the East, and the South as well, occupying mostly lower skilled jobs. More than 25 percent of the Mexican-born have arrived since 2000. Coinciding with this influx has been the development of fierce partisan positions about whether to legalize, or proffer paths for legalization to, undocumented immigrants. At the present time it seems that the Republican Party is favored by Americans who want to curtail immigration and deny any form of amnesty for undocumented immigrants while the Democratic Party seeks ways to assist some of them blend in with American society.

What follows in these chapters is an account of the different groups of immigrants who have contributed to the prosperity of the United States since the end of World War II: what the circumstances of their arrival were, what American needs were, and how, collectively, they helped propel American economic growth. Moreover, for most of the well-educated or highly skilled newcomers, economic and social opportunities abounded. Both the immigrants and the Americans have continued the traditions established in the British colonies in the seventeenth century. No other nation in the world has welcomed, transformed, and absorbed so many different ethnic strains into one large population, most of whose members are proud to call themselves "American."

CHAPTER 1

The Fruits of War, Hot and Cold

Immigration, 1945–1965

As a result of World War II the United States became an active participant in world affairs. Along with wartime allies Great Britain and the Soviet Union, the United States and its leader, President Franklin Delano Roosevelt, pushed for the establishment of an international organization in which the major powers would lead other countries in the attempt to maintain world peace. The world's leading nations established the United Nations, convened just days after Roosevelt's death in April 1945. With the beginning of the Cold War in 1946, America increased its military presence in Europe by joining with Western European nations to oppose the expansion of communism. Immigration had a vital connection to these political and military affairs, which indirectly led the United States to rethink existing policies.

As the hostilities came to an end the United States faced the over thirty million Europeans dislocated by war. About a million people labeled "displaced persons" or "DPs," remained homeless and created a major problem for the allies who were eager to rebuild Germany. The DPs had been removed from their homelands during the war and either would, or could, not return to their native lands in Eastern Europe. Their plight differed vastly from those faced by refugees before the war whose lives were in peril.

After the war other nations expected the United States to lead in solving the world's existing problems. That included helping to find homes for the survivors who gathered in camp-like settings waiting to receive assistance in resettlement. Most of the DPs sought entry into countries outside of Germany and Eastern Europe, but most of the nations where they wanted to go either did not want them or would accept only token numbers. In 1945 the United States urged its allies in Europe and the Western Hemisphere to accommodate the refugees, but neither Congress nor President Harry S. Truman showed any inclination to bend existing American quota laws.

Almost all of the other countries affected by the war, mostly in Europe and Asia, needed outside help to regroup, rebuild their societies, and reignite their economies. Thus the United States became deeply involved politically and militarily with most of the nations in Western Europe and Asia, but its rigidity in refusing to welcome a "fair share" of DPs complicated foreign relations, especially with Great Britain. Both the German and Japanese empires had been decimated, European nations were about to disintegrate and lose their colonies in Asia and Africa, and the Soviet Union had lost nearly twenty-five million people during the war. Asian nations, too, had suffered during the war, as millions were killed and uprooted, especially in China. Japan also lost several million soldiers, and two of its cities, Hiroshima and Nagasaki, were destroyed by atomic bombs. Although the United States established a military occupation of Japan, it paid less attention to Asia than it did to Europe. Perhaps the primary reason for the intense focus on Europe was concern about the totalitarian nature of Soviet communism and fears that the Soviet Union intended to engulf all of Europe.

Major ideological barriers also developed in 1945, and this, too, affected immigration policies. The United States and the Soviet Union entered a Cold War, created by the respective ideologies of each nation. The United States proclaimed its belief in capitalism and democracy, whereas the Soviet Union favored political authoritarianism and government ownership of the major means of production. Both nations influenced the politics and economies of their satellites and allies: the Soviets in Eastern Europe and the United States in Western Europe and Latin America. Both nations feared the influence of the other major power on their citizens and both tried to limit contact between communists and capitalists. Because of these anxieties Congress erected barriers to prevent people entering the United States from communist nations unless they had strongly indicated that they were repudiating the Soviet's tyrannical philosophy. On the other hand, some Americans did not regard former Nazis from Germany as undesirable persons.

In the 1950s and 1960s Hungarians and Cubans received special consideration that allowed them to enter the United States. The former because they rebelled against a communist government; the latter because a communist took over their government, nationalized private businesses, and appeared to be cementing relations with the Soviet Union, which the United States believed threatened harmonious relations throughout the world.

From the early 1940s through the late 1960s most newcomers to the United States came from Great Britain, Italy, Germany, Canada, and Mexico. In fact, Mexicans were recruited as guest workers ("Braceros") during World War II, and afterward major domestic agricultural interests in the Southwest used their political influence to continue the program. Business leaders favored the use of cheap temporary labor. English-speaking and well-educated Canadian immigrants generally faded into the American scene wherever they went. French Canadians, on the other hand, like almost all of the laborers from Mexico, were less well educated, sought whatever kind of work they could find, and generally settled in the factory towns and rural areas of all of the New England states except Connecticut.

THE WAR BRIDES

The first immigration issue facing policy makers in 1945 was that many of the foreign-born spouses of members of the US armed forces faced formidable immigrant quotas and exclusions. Members of Congress, recognizing the need to resolve this issue quickly, passed the War Brides Act of 1945. The new bill facilitated a process for European-born family members to join American spouses in the United States. The first ship, the *SS Argentina* left England with 451 women and 175 children in January 1946 and received great fanfare in the US press. Two-thirds of all Americans favored the War Brides Act, and in 1946 Congress amended the bill to include several thousand Chinese -born women and children. Special laws passed later allowed Japanese and Korean women married to American soldiers to enter.

Few husbands of American female veterans came to the United States as a result of the Act. The immigration authorities reported in 1949 that they had admitted 117,999 wives and children of United States members of the armed services but only 327 husbands of military women. However, female veterans were less likely to meet and marry foreign men because so few women were stationed overseas and female military personnel had their movements carefully monitored. Regulations prevented most servicewomen from leaving their bases for recreational purposes without a companion or chaperone.

In and near military bases, regulations were often issued regarding whom soldiers might fraternize with and which areas in a community were off limits. Sometimes social relationships with military personnel and community inhabitants were prohibited. In fact, these edicts were often ignored or difficult to enforce. Nonetheless they existed. Polls in 1945 and 1946 indicated that the GIs felt kindly toward the German people as opposed to Nazi leaders. The army worried about the prevalence of venereal disease among US troops and came to believe that it was better for American soldiers to meet "respectable" German women rather than those who could be picked up on the streets. As a result, by 1946 the military commanders permitted Americans to date and even marry German women.

Military commanders also claimed the right to approve of marriages between their subordinates and non-Americans. Again, this "right" was pro forma but could be enforced. Thus most Americans overseas had no difficulty marrying people with whom they fell in love or qualifying to bring their spouses to the United States. However, racism played a factor in obtaining permission to do so. It was one thing for white soldiers to marry Europeans, but black soldiers who made similar choices found approval from their military commanders difficult to obtain. World War II was fought with a racially segregated army, and interracial marriage was uncommon in the United States in the 1940s and 1950s. Many states prohibited such unions; not until 1967 did the US Supreme Court rule these laws unconstitutional. Military authorities insisted it was not the business of the army to force social changes at home. Returning African American GIs who were able to bring their white wives with them encountered a highly disapproving society.

AN IMMIGRANT'S TALE

Joy Davis met her future husband, Wilbur "Web" Davis, while working with the voluntary English Women's Land Army and Timber Corps. When they met in 1944, she was going to mail a letter and was covered with dirt and hay and even cow dung. He was riding a bicycle and asked her why she was going so fast. From that meeting the couple began their courtship. When they married, she became one of the British war brides.

"The war changed my life," she recalled. She had never worked on a farm until she met her future spouse. She was only eighteen, but when they met and fell in love, they decided to marry nonetheless. She arrived in the United States on July 12, 1946, and the couple was married four days later. That was the worst time to come to the United States, she recalled, as the heat was terrible. "It wasn't that way in England." Many war brides were homesick, but in Joy's case she was fortunate because a mailman helped her meet other war brides, who formed an Anglo-American club in Boone, Iowa, where the couple had settled. Her experience was a good one. She recounted that she was well received by the community and their reception made the transition from Great Britain to the United States easier than it was for many other war brides.

The couple raised three children and celebrated their sixtieth anniversary in 2006, shortly before her husband died. Looking back she said, "If I hadn't gone to the Land Army, I never would have met him. Our paths never would have crossed. I probably would have just done ledgers at the bank for the rest of my life." Not all such marriages ended so well. Many war brides were plagued by homesickness and the stress eventually led to divorces.

THE DISPLACED PERSONS ACT

The postwar changes in American immigration policy were closely tied to the programs designed to rebuild Western Europe and combat communism. In September 1945 there were perhaps a million DPs in central Europe who either could, or would, not return to their prewar homes. About 5 to 10 percent of these people were Jews from Eastern Europe. Despite their relatively small number they received disproportionate publicity because of their horrendous wartime experiences and the desire of so many of them to resettle either in the United States or Palestine. Under a previous League of Nations mandate, Great Britain controlled Palestine. The British granted entry to a relatively small number of Jews in order to remain friendly with the Arab powers controlling the region's oil. On the other hand, American Zionists and their domestic allies bombarded President Truman with missiles demanding admission of the European Jews to Palestine. American Jews voted overwhelmingly for the Democratic Party and provided much of its financing. Truman recognized the need to placate them.

As a partial solution to the plight of the growing numbers of Jewish displaced persons in Europe, President Truman ordered the State Department to favor DPs when filling existing European immigration quotas. Known as the Truman Directive, this resulted in 35,000–41,000 displaced European Jews receiving visas to enter the United States between the date it was issued, December 22, 1945, and June 30, 1948. More than any other religious group, Jews benefited from the Truman Directive because Jewish agencies were quicker to assist DPs with both financial and technical assistance. They filled out applications, gathered appropriate documents, and facilitated connections between Jewish DPs and American sponsors. Christian social agencies at that time believed, despite published statistics to the contrary, that most DPs were Jewish and therefore they made little effort to resettle the displaced persons or to call for enlarged immigration quotas. Anti-Semitism was prevalent in the United States at that time, and most Americans opposed bringing more Jews to America.

The Christian social agencies' views reflected prevailing attitudes. Most Americans had not changed their basic opposition to admitting non-WASP immigrants since the 1920s, and members of Congress reflected their constituents' sentiments. In 1945 Eleanor Roosevelt, the president's widow, wrote that she had not spoken with a single member of Congress who wanted more generous immigration laws. During World War II and immediately afterward several patriotic organizations, including the American Legion, the Veterans of Foreign Wars, and the Daughters of the American Revolution (DAR), called for total bans on all future immigration for periods of five to ten years. A 1946 Gallup Poll found that 51 percent of Americans opposed increasing immigration quotas; 32 percent supported the status quo; and only 5 percent favored bringing additional foreigners to the United States.

Jews in the United States realized that opposition to receiving DPs related closely to existing anti-Semitism. Therefore, they helped form a new lobbying organization, the Citizens Committee on Displaced Persons (CCDP), to educate the public and work for legal changes to admit at least 100,000 Jewish DPs. In its publications and contacts with politicians, the CCDP continually reiterated that 80 percent of the DP population was Christian, which was true, and rarely discussed the presence of Jews among those seeking entry to the United States. Once Christian groups recognized that the overwhelming number of DPs were not Jewish, they joined efforts with the CCDP to seek changes in existing immigration laws. In response to the combined pressure, Congress passed a bill in June 1948 that called for the admission of 205,000 DPs.

Unfortunately the CCDP did not achieve its publicly unstated desired goal: bringing 100,000 DP Jews to the United States. The bill Congress passed deliberately discriminated against Jews and favored both Christians and even former

Nazis. The act called for admission of DPs who had registered with allied forces in Germany when the Truman Directive was issued on December 22, 1945. However, about 150,000 Jewish DPs who had fled to the Soviet Union during World War II were ineligible for consideration because they were not allowed to leave that country until the spring of 1946. Furthermore, the bill required allocation of at least 30 percent of all visas to people "previously engaged in agricultural pursuits." It was well known in Congress during the time of the bill's consideration that only 2 percent of the Jewish DPs had previously engaged in agricultural pursuits. Finally, special provisions were made for the Eastern European ethnic Germans who had been expelled from their homes after World War II because many had supported the Nazis during the war. For members of this group to qualify for admission, they only needed to register in the US-run DP camps by July 1, 1948, a week after the president signed the bill. In 1950 Congress eliminated this legislation's discriminatory features and offered admission to another 200,000 DPs who had registered with American authorities by April 1947.

Passage of the 1948 Displaced Persons Act had far-reaching implications. Setting a precedent, it was the first law to make specific provision for refugees and homeless persons when considering admittance to the United States. Refugees constituted about one-fifth of all immigrants coming to the United States between 1946 and 1965. The act was also important because it brought together different ethnic and religious groups. For some American Jews, it was the first time they engaged in a common cause with Gentiles. During their work together a general feeling developed that United States immigration policy needed to be rethought and rewritten.

JEWISH DISPLACED PERSONS

While the literature on the adaptation of most of the Christian DPs who came to the United States is thin, Jewish DPs wrote more extensively of their bittersweet memories. Although most eventually adjusted to life in the United States, their wartime trials and tribulations often left permanent physical and emotional scars. Many recalled tales of horror that few US citizens could comprehend. One DP told his son that he had been afraid to return to Poland when the war ended because the Poles "might kill him for sport." Those who did return to their prewar homes seeking relatives and friends often experienced frightening and bizarre encounters. Their property had been confiscated, and the new "owners" refused to return it. They were asked by former neighbors, "Are you still alive? What are you doing here?" Subsequent pogroms in Poland during 1945–1946 left few Jews with a desire to remain in that country. When the opportunity to go to United States appeared, surviving Jews lucky enough to qualify for visas took them. Once they were in the United States the basic needs of the former DPs were met but their psyches were scarred. Many of the people they met could not relate to their tales of misery.

Although Holocaust survivors were hurt and humiliated by the insensitive and negative reactions they encountered, they rarely indulged in self-pity. Instead, they took advantage of existing opportunities. Most survivors made great efforts to learn English, often self-conscious about their accents and mispronunciations. Given a chance to work, they did. The men, and many times their wives, found jobs in poorly paying industries that offered opportunities to develop marketable skills as upholsterers, dress makers, or shoe repairmen. They worked long hours in jobs far lower in status than the ones they had held before the war. For most, working proved therapeutic, focusing their minds on the tasks at hands. Many families saved their incomes wisely, and soon began to purchases businesses of their own.

Several aspects of life in the United States contributed to the speed of adjustment. Most of the newcomers either set up or joined supportive communities. Over two-thirds of the Jewish DPs remained in New York, then the city with the world's largest Jewish population. Having supportive relatives, jobs, Yiddish newspapers, and a circle of friends with similar experiences quickened the pace of adaptation. For religious Jews, finding an appropriate orthodox synagogue and a friendly rabbi enhanced their sense of well-being. Another factor that, in retrospect, seems to have been a determinant was their childhood experiences. Although all the DPs had shared the horrors of war, those who had been nurtured in their youth did not find the process of adjustment as difficult as did people who had troubled childhoods.

Toward the end of the 1970s, after knowledge of the Holocaust spread, the former DPs were celebrated and respected as heroes. By the 1980s a collective portrait of survivors in the United States showed that they had higher than average per capita incomes. Most worked or had worked as craftsmen or in semiprofessional, managerial, sales, or clerical positions. In 1989, 83 percent of them were still married (80 percent to other survivors) in contrast to 62 percent of other American Jews in their age group. More than 40 percent of these former refugees identified themselves as religious, compared to 10 percent of Jews born in the United States. They were grateful for the opportunities that they had received in their adopted country. In her twilight years, one survivor admitted that after the war it took time "for me to understand how there could ever be a luxury greater than bread; but most of all, to have this liberty. I cannot tell you what it meant to us to come to America; this was the freedom we had never known before. To speak freely, to be without fear, to think as you like. It did not take us long to see what this country was. Americans do not know, they cannot understand what they have here."

OTHER EUROPEAN NONQUOTA
IMMIGRANTS AND REFUGEES

While Jews had difficulty qualifying for admission as immigrants after the first DP Act, Christian nationals from Eastern European nations did not. Lithuanians and the Balts are good examples. Lithuania had been invaded by the Soviets at the beginning of World War II in 1939. The Soviet army arrested and killed thousands of Lithuanians. In June 1941 the Nazis invaded the Soviet Union and German troops replaced the Russian occupying forces. As World War II came to an end, the Soviet army once again occupied Lithuania and the Baltic states. Rather than face further Russian domination, many Estonians, Latvians, and Lithuanians fled to Western Europe. The Lithuanian quota for immigration to the United States was only 384, but under the provisions stipulated in the displaced persons acts of 1948 and 1950 over 27,000 Lithuanians arrived in the United States. In addition, several thousand more Lithuanians, other Balts, Italians, Greeks, and Portuguese migrated to the United States under the Refugee Relief Act of 1953 or other acts designed to help European groups. Rhode Island Senator John Pastore (D), the first person of Italian heritage to sit in the US Senate, along with Senator John F. Kennedy (D, MA) and others, sponsored legislation in 1958 to admit fifteen hundred people from the Azores, and four years later offered another bill, which allowed sixteen thousand southern European siblings of US citizens to enter the country (see Table 1.1).

One group of Germans expelled from some Eastern European countries presented a problem. Many Europeans and Americans regarded them as Nazis, which may or may not have been true. Most of them arrived in America with little fanfare. Thousands of these newcomers were not proud of everything that they had done during the war and its aftermath, and did not want their past behavior scrutinized. Some had been Nazis, others had engaged in slaughtering noncombatants, and some just wanted to remain anonymous and live out the rest of their lives quietly. It was generally believed that as many as ten thousand Nazis were accepted as immigrants by officials of government intelligence programs who wanted to use their knowledge of European communism, but a federal government report in 2010 indicated that the figure was smaller. However, other Nazis had either lied on their applications for admission or used loopholes in the immigration laws to enter the United States.

To avoid being lumped together in the US imagination as Nazis, German immigrants tended to spread out across the country, and generally avoided talking about their wartime experiences. Moreover, many younger Germans felt they had

Table 1.1 Postwar Refugees, 1945–1965

COUNTRY OR REGION OF BIRTH	NUMBER OF REFUGEES
Poland	154,000
Austria-Germany (includes Germans born in other nations)	168,000
Baltic States (Estonia, Latvia, Lithuania)	74,000
Italy	62,000
Yugoslavia	45,000
Hungary	60,000
United Soviet Socialist Republics (USSR)	38,000
Greece	28,000
Romania	21,000

SOURCE: Immigration and Naturalization Service, *Annual Reports*, 1945–1965.

nothing to connect them to the war, and they did not wish to bring attention to themselves. For almost twenty years they were successful in this endeavor.

In the 1960s, many Americans began questioning issues that had not formerly been examined. One concerned the activities some of these immigrants had engaged in during World War II. In the 1970s the United States responded to the requests of Israel and Germany to return immigrants accused of participating in the Nazi slaughter of almost six million Jews during the war. The number of alleged culprits was not large, but they did point to the lax screening processes for European immigrants after the war.

Perhaps the most sensational case, and certainly the longest, was that of John Demjankuk. After the war he immigrated to the United States and became an American citizen in 1952, working at an auto plant for years. The Israelis insisted that he was the notorious guard, "Ivan the Terrible," at Treblinka Concentration Camp. He was stripped of his US citizenship in 1981, when authorities claimed he had concealed his past as a Nazi death camp guard. He was extradited to Israel a few years later, put on trial, and convicted by an Israeli court of crimes against humanity. However, confusion about the evidence leading to his conviction resulted in his release and return to the United States. His citizenship was restored in 1998, only to be revoked again in 2002. The German government stated that it had new data that Demjankuk, who had been born in the Ukraine, had committed crimes at Sobibor and other death camps. Demjankuk claimed that he was taken prisoner by the Germans and held as a prisoner of war and had not participated in any criminal activity. In 2009 Demjankuk was again expelled from the United States and repatriated to Germany to face war crimes charges. By then Demjankuk was ninety years old, in frail health, and was barely able to stand trial. Nonetheless, in 2011 he was convicted. He died in a nursing home in Germany in March 2012.

THE McCARRAN-WALTER ACT
AND IMMIGRATION IN THE 1950s

Because the United States was in a Cold War with the Soviet Union it did not serve the nation's purposes, or improve America's image abroad, when the Soviets continually pointed out how the United States chose immigrants on the basis of ethnicity. Such choices were both racist and discriminatory. Although Congress was in no mood to enact far-reaching changes, legislators decided to reconsider the immigration laws.

In 1947 the Senate Judiciary Committee had begun a deep and comprehensive study of the nation's immigration policies. The culmination of that study resulted in the passage of the McCarran-Walter Act in 1952. Neither Senator Pat McCarran (D, NV) nor Representative Francis Walter (D, PA) favored significant changes to existing legislation. They read the public temper well and knew how little support there was for altering the existing quota system. While McCarran had supported the admission of war brides, including Asians, after World War II, he opposed entry of practically all other immigrants, except for 250 Basque sheep herders from Spain and France in 1950 who were desperately needed in his home state.

There were a few other noteworthy aspects of the legislation. One provided a quota allotment of at least one hundred persons to every nation in the Eastern Hemisphere. This provision eliminated the ban against Asian immigration. Although two thousand annual quota slots were established for all Asians, spouses and minor children of US citizens were not included in that number, an exemption that proved beneficial for people from many nations then and in the future. A second improvement of the McCarran-Walter Act erased gender differences in bringing spouses and their children as immigrants and allowed men and women the same opportunities. The McCarran-Walter Act also established two new principles. First, it defined refugees as persons fleeing or escaping from communism; in previous legislation the term "refugee" had not been defined. The United States would continue to use this strict definition until passage of the Refugee Act of 1980. Also, within this legislation Congress specifically called for the admission of two identifiable groups of people: Middle Eastern and Asian refugees.

Otherwise, the McCarran-Walter Act perpetuated the discriminatory features of the 1924 Immigration Act, and it established a quota of only one hundred for present and former British colonies in the West Indies. The bill also expanded officials' power to bar aliens suspected of communist sympathies. Because of the continuation of the national origins quota system favoring Western Europe, and the xenophobic aspects written into the legislation, President Truman vetoed the bill. He called it "about the worst piece of legislation that has ever been placed on the books," but a two-thirds majority in Congress quickly overrode his objections. Later in the decade, *The Saturday Evening Post*, the most mainstream American publication at that time, underscored Congress' decision. It expressed what was probably the majority opinion in "middle America": "we must hold fast to our policy [national origins system] so that the cultural characteristics of our population will not be materially altered."

General Dwight D. Eisenhower, a Republican who won an overwhelming victory in the presidential election of 1952, also wanted alterations in the McCarran-Walter Act. For both humanitarian and political reasons, the new president favored additional legislation to bring in more anticommunist refugees from southeast Europe. Supporters of this position also stressed the importance of easing Europe's overpopulation problem. It was claimed that because many Europeans lacked adequate homes, jobs, and hope, they were liable to find communism attractive. Congress responded to the president's request by passing the Refugee Relief Act of 1953, which called for the admission of 214,000 persons. But suspicious anticommunist administrative officials in the State Department dragged their feet and processed the refugees' paperwork slowly.

ANTICOMMUNISM AND EUROPEAN ADMISSIONS

Anticommunism featured prominently in the escape of two hundred thousand refugees who fled to Austria following the abortive anticommunist Hungarian

Revolution of 1956. In the intense atmosphere of the Cold War, the United States aired propaganda broadcasts from the "Voice of America" radio to European nations under communist domination, extolling the virtues of life under democracy and capitalism. Many Europeans heard about this promised good life in the west and were eager to escape. Eastern Germans, Poles, and Czechs managed to do so, but no other group succeeded as well as the refugees who fled their homelands during the 1956 Hungarian Revolution.

Thousands of Hungarians believed that the United States not only encouraged them to revolt but had promised assistance as well. Whether such promises were actually made is difficult to document, but Hungarians took to the streets in November 1956, calling for an end to its communist government. Soviet troops and tanks easily crushed the uprising, but over two hundred thousand Hungarians escaped to Austria before the border was sealed. Austrians insisted that they could not care for so many new arrivals.

Approximately fifteen hundred Hungarians a year might have qualified for entry into the United States under existing quotas. However, one of the provisions of the McCarran-Walter Act granted power to the US attorney general to "parole" individuals into the country in emergency situations. President Eisenhower believed that the Hungarian crisis qualified as an emergency situation and instructed his attorney general to exercise his congressionally given authority to parole thirty-eight thousand Hungarian refugees. By doing so the Eisenhower administration established a precedent that succeeding presidents seized on to admit hundreds of thousands of other refugees, especially Cubans and South Asians.

Once Hungarians began arriving, the federal government staged a campaign to celebrate the brave "Freedom Fighters" who resisted communism. Popular periodicals promoted the virtues of the Hungarians, who, they asserted, were acculturating quickly. *Life* magazine related the tale of one family who resettled in Indianapolis. They sent their children to public schools, attended church, were learning English, watched American television, and showed every indication that they were quickly becoming part of an American culture. Readers of *Life* also saw pictures of Hungarian-born schoolchildren pledging allegiance to the American flag. Indeed, they seemed like ideal citizens.

Anticommunist intellectuals, students, and political protesters figured prominently among those admitted to the United States, but many of the arriving Hungarians were primarily interested in securing a better economic life for themselves and their families. Among the Hungarian refugees were thousands of well-educated individuals including scientists, doctors, and engineers. Some of them spoke several European languages, but few handled English well. The federal government brought the "Freedom Fighters" to Camp Kilmer, New Jersey, to facilitate the newcomers' adjustment; they were provided with many helpful services including the teaching of English. The National Academy of Science helped place the elite in positions consistent with their educations. Congress backed President Eisenhower's decision to parole the Hungarians by subsequently voting to change their status from refugees to immigrants.

AN IMMIGRANT'S TALE

Bela Kiraly was perhaps the most famous of the Hungarian "Freedom Fighters" of 1956. Born in 1912, he joined the Hungarian army in 1930 and during World War II he served on the eastern front. His most notable action during the war was to save several hundred Jews from concentration camps by making them soldiers. Saving them from the camps in this way meant that the new Jewish soldiers would not automatically be killed; life in the Hungarian army gave them some chance for survival. For this action, the Israelis called him a "righteous Gentile." Promoted under the communists who took over his country at the end of World War II, General Kiraly became the founding commander of the Zrinyi Miklos National Defense University.

However, he soon lost the support of the new communist regime in Hungary, and in 1950 was arrested and condemned to death. The sentence was not carried out, and he served only five years in prison. Kiraly was released just at the time of the Hungarian Revolution of 1956. Although Kiraly was in poor health after his years in prison, the leader of the revolt, Prime Minister Imre Nagy, appointed him leader of the anti-Soviet military forces. The "Freedom Fighters" were no match for the Soviet troops. The Russians quickly defeated these revolutionary forces, leading to the exodus of two hundred thousand Hungarians into neighboring Austria. Kiraly was among those who escaped. The American Central Intelligence Agency (CIA) helped Kiraly obtain asylum in the United States.

He then earned a Ph.D. at Columbia University and taught history at Brooklyn College in New York City until his retirement. When communism collapsed in his homeland, he returned and became a folk hero. Kiraly was elected a member of the Hungarian parliament and served from 1990 to 1994. He died in 2009.

As the Cold War intensified, however, potential refugees living in communist-controlled Eastern Europe found it difficult to escape. For many years thousands of East Germans had crossed into democratic West Berlin without difficulty. The Soviets abruptly ended that flow by erecting a wall, during the night of August 12–13, 1961, dividing the city. Some Germans who escaped from the East migrated to the United States. And in 1968 the Czechoslovakian government's repression of political protesters similarly propelled a mass departure as thousands more also sought refuge in the United States.

THE QUOTA EUROPEAN IMMIGRANTS

Half of the post–World War II European immigrants came to the United States under the quota system established in 1924. English, German, and Irish natives had been given the largest number of slots in the 1924 immigration act, and they constituted a majority of foreigners who settled in the United States after the war. Including refugees, Germany alone sent nearly six hundred thousand immigrants during the 1950s.

The migration of scientists and professionals stood out as a prominent feature of British and German immigration from 1946 to 1965. While European economies struggled to revive after World War II, the United States invested in national defense, suburban expansion, consumer goods, space exploration, and health-related programs. Under "Operation Paperclip" 765 German scientists and engineers were brought to the United States shortly after the end of World War II. During the war many of them had been involved with the German weapons program, which had produced V-2 rockets that were used against Great Britain. When the war ended, the German scientists who still remained in Europe feared being captured by the Russians. They believed that the harsh living and working conditions prevailing in the Soviet Union would curtail their professional opportunities, and, when possible, they preferred to surrender to the Americans. Those who succeeded in doing so were later brought to a military camp near El Paso, Texas. They eventually moved to Huntsville, Alabama, where they made important contributions to the development of space exploration and rockets.

Most of the immigrants with scientific and other professional credentials came into the United States under the regular national origin quotas. Their entry was made easier because, within the quotas, preference was given to family members and persons needed to aid the US economy. Between 1949 and 1965 the immigration of engineers quadrupled and the number of scientists grew five times. In 1949 the number of immigrant physicians recorded was 1,148; in 1965 the figure was 2,249. In 1950 only 5 percent of new medical licenses in the United States went to graduates of foreign birth; ten years later that figure had risen to 18 percent.

By 1965, 20 percent of foreign-born scientists and engineers in the United States came from the United Kingdom. The exodus of so many British-trained scientific and professional personnel alarmed members of Britain's Royal Society, who termed this a "brain drain." In 1957 a British report declared, "The [British] government, by the millions spent on technical education, were merely erecting a vast and expensive preparatory school for American industry."

The flight of their most highly educated persons to the United States alarmed other European nations as well. Some leaders dubbed the departure "a Marshall Plan in reverse" with the Europeans providing highly educated immigrants to the American economy. These new immigrants provided important benefits to the United States and were recognized for their striking accomplishments. In 1961 the National Academy of Sciences noted that among its members 24 percent were foreign-born.

Some other immigrants had been trained in crafts needed in the United States. At first, they had trouble obtaining jobs because of their inability to read and write English. On the whole, however, the Europeans who arrived between 1945 and 1965 were able to make the necessary adjustments to blend in with American workers. The average incomes of the people who came during these two decades caught up to those of native-born Americans within fifteen years of their arrival. These people were also fortunate to reach America during an era of great economic expansion when the United States reigned as the world's dominant power.

NEW ASIAN IMMIGRANTS

No other demographic shift in US immigration policy was more noticeable than with Asians. Asians had been victimized by intense racism in the United States until well past the end of World War II. Nonetheless, efforts to change American policy began during the war. As a gesture to a wartime ally, in 1943 Congress lifted an existing restriction and gave China a quota of 105. Three years later Congress amended the War Brides Act and allowed about six thousand Chinese women to emigrate and join their husbands. Filipino men who enlisted in the American army also were permitted to naturalize.

Between the end of World War II and 1993 the United States maintained military bases in the Philippines. Several thousand servicemen met and married Filipino women, and after their tour of duty ended, they brought their wives stateside. After 1952, all Asians married to American citizens could immigrate to the United States without concern about quota restrictions.

Unlike in Europe, where US troops occupied Germany along with their wartime allies, in Japan the American government assumed complete control. Roughly one million servicemen saw duty in Japan from 1945 to 1952. At first many Japanese civilians feared Americans because they had believed their government's propaganda that occupying forces would treat them brutally. Both Caucasian and Japanese American soldiers fraternized with local people, although it was easier for Japanese American troops to marry Japanese women. Special laws enacted by Congress permitted Japanese war brides to enter, until the McCarran-Walter Immigration Act eliminated the need for exceptions.

Although the exact number of unions between servicemen and Japanese women is not known, there were enough that the Red Cross established "bride schools" in Japan featuring English-language classes and instruction in American folkways and mores. These "schools" helped several thousand Japanese-born women who arrived annually in the United States. It is estimated that by 1975 more than 66,681 Japanese immigrant women had reached American shores.

Korean women also joined the ranks of foreigners who married American servicemen. Over five hundred thousand American soldiers served in Korea during the war that began in 1950, and afterward the United States maintained military forces in South Korea. Fraternization between troops and Korean women was a concomitant result of the occupation. Liaisons were facilitated by bars and houses of prostitution, called "Camptowns," which surrounded military bases. Koreans regarded women working in such places as outcasts. Other Korean women became familiar with US citizens through their employment at the military post exchanges (PX), where a great variety of consumer goods were available to Americans. It is not known how many marriages between US men and Korean women resulted from these associations. In 1953, the year of the truce, 100 Korean wives left for the United States; six years later the total reached 488. Precise figures after that date are not available but over eleven thousand Korean War Brides reached the United States in the 1960s, and many more came later.

Once in the United States, many Asian women faced discrimination. As noted, interracial marriage in the United States was not common and was illegal in many states in the 1940s and 1950s. The historian Susan Geiger wrote that evidence of bigotry toward Asian war brides is lacking, but many women reported that racial segregation and discrimination were common. One Filipina, who had married an African American, recalled that where the couple settled in Virginia "the discrimination was terrible." The civil rights movement of the late 1950s and 1960s made intermarriage more respectable, and, as noted, a 1967 Supreme Court decision struck down legal barriers against interracial marriage. Intermarriage rates grew sharply after the 1980s. Nonetheless, many Asian war brides had a hard time adjusting to racial mores in the United States.

Marriage to American soldiers and sailors does not alone explain how Asian immigration grew after the end of World War II. Some Asians entered as refugees exempt from national quotas. When the communists won control of the Chinese government in 1949, several thousand Chinese scholars were working in the United States. They did not wish to return home, and in the 1950s the American government permitted them to remain as immigrants. Using the parole power President Eisenhower had employed for Hungarians, President John F. Kennedy allowed fifteen thousand Chinese refugees from Hong Kong to come to the United States in the early 1960s. Overall over 30,000 Chinese refugees were admitted between 1948 and 1965, and some of these highly educated Chinese went on to develop exceptional careers. These refugees represented only a tiny fraction of the million Chinese who fled the Red Army, but they were meant as a token of America's commitment to the Far East.

ANTICOMMUNIST CUBANS

The Cold War also shaped immigration policies for people closer to home. In 1958 Fidel Castro's successful revolutionary struggle overthrew the repressive regime of Fulgencio Batista in Cuba. At first Castro's aims were not clear and the US responses to the new Cuba were ill-defined. Later, when Castro announced that he was a communist and nationalized both native and foreign businesses, relations between the two nations soured. As a result of having their businesses and other properties confiscated, waves of middle- and upper-class Cubans left for the United States. The initial exodus from the island began in 1959 and included a disproportionately large number of white, skilled, college-educated, white collar, and managerial professionals. Many of these "golden exiles," as they were later called, settled in Florida, where they became quite successful. A large number of these elite were familiar with the area. They had vacationed, done business, or had relatives and friends in Miami and the state of Florida. Overall, several hundred thousand refugees fled Cuba before the Soviet Union installed missiles on the island in August 1962. The American government considered these weapons a threat to the nation's security and demanded that they be removed. To prevent another war the Soviets capitulated. For the next three years air connections between Cuba and Miami ceased. However, in 1965 Castro indicated that he would allow all Cubans desirous of leaving the nation to do so. President Lyndon B. Johnson then announced that they would be welcome in the United States.

In 1966 Congress passed the Cuban Adjustment Act, which gave any Cuban who reached the United States the right of refuge, provided the individual was not on the list of those banned, such as criminals or persons with certain diseases. The Cuban Adjustment Act spurred other islanders to seek refuge on American soil. Three waves of Cubans arrived. One, mostly white and lower middle class, came during the years 1965–1973; a second, largely black and working class, arrived in 1980; and a third, much smaller group, called the "rafters" because of their mode of transportation, reached the United States in 1994. Moreover, Congress authorized funds to aid the Cubans in their adjustment to the United States.

The initial group of Cuban refugees who arrived shortly after Castro assumed power turned the sleepy city of Miami into a vibrant Hispanic community. One Cuban woman who had settled there in 1949 recalled, "Downtown Miami was three blocks. The courthouse was there, and there were no big buildings. The banks and all that came later. Miami at this time was nothing. It was a suburb of Miami Beach." In the 1960s Miami emerged as a key city in the United States' connection to Latin America. Spanish flourished as the language of business: "Aqui se habla espanol" signs appeared in store windows; and one could hear Spanish on the streets, in coffee houses, and at Cuban cultural events.

Thousands of Cubans arrived in the United States with little money and had to begin working at menial tasks. Nonetheless, their savvy, work ethic, and willingness to take chances propelled them into the middle class at a faster rate than members of any other immigrant group since the French Huguenots arrived in the British colonies in the 1680s. Most Americans admired these Cubans because they worked hard and opposed communism. Of course many Cubans did well precisely because of their education and contacts. One successful Cuban American who became quite wealthy was Roberto Goizueta. A Yale graduate who worked for Coca Cola in Cuba, he left the island with practically nothing in his pockets. In the United States, he resumed working for Coca Cola. By the early 1980s, he had risen to the top of the corporation.

At first these Cuban immigrants did not think of themselves as Americans. Rather they were hopeful of returning to their island homes after Fidel Castro and communism were replaced. Some Cubans in the United States participated in an attempt to overthrow Castro's government by invading Cuba's Bay of Pigs in 1961. Though the invasion, backed by the Central Intelligence Agency (CIA), proved to be a disaster, many Cubans still longed for the day when Castro would no longer reign. With the passage of time, however, his demise appeared unlikely. Even when illness forced the dictator to turn over control of the government to a younger brother in 2007, Americans of Cuban ancestry made no efforts to overthrow the new regime. The younger generations of Cuban Americans grew up in the United States, had little interest in foreign policy, and identified themselves as Americans of Cuban heritage, not as Cubans in exile.

OTHER IMMIGRATION FROM
THE WESTERN HEMISPHERE

Most immigrants from the Western Hemisphere were not refugees from communism. Rather, they were largely motivated by the dream of a better life in the world's richest and most dominant nation. The largest two groups were from Canada and Mexico. Both of these nations were not hindered by quotas, because individual Western Hemisphere nations, except for West Indians, lacked quotas until the 1970s. Of course Mexicans and Canadians had to meet immigration regulations such as passing a literacy test, paying a head tax, and being free of certain diseases. As a result of the relatively open immigration policies for Canada and Mexico, immigration from those countries grew during the late 1940s and 1950s. Canadians constituted the largest number of immigrants from any one Western Hemisphere nation in those years, but in the 1960s Mexican immigration levels surpassed those of Canadians. Table 1.2 indicates migration totals of people reaching the United States from the 1940s through the 1960s. The figures include refugees.

Most Canadian newcomers assimilated easily. Unlike the period before World War II, when the bulk of Canadians were French speakers of rural and/or working-class background, the post-1945 Canadian immigrants were mostly well-educated English speakers. Of those with occupations, professionals constituted one-fourth of the group and skilled workers another fourth. These Canadians, like many English and Germans, were part of the "brain drain" to the United States that characterized the immediate postwar era. (In a later period the "brain drain" would include more Asians and Africans.) Canadian officials, like their counterparts in

Table 1.2 Sources of Immigration from Four Nations

	1940–1949	1950–1959	1960–1969
Germany	119,506	575,905	209,616
United Kingdom	131,794	195,709	220,213
Mexico	56,158	273,847	441,824
Canada	160,911	353,169	433,128

SOURCE: Office of Statistics, US Department of Homeland Security, *Statistical Yearbook*, 2008.

Europe, worried that many of their citizens were leaving the country for better employment opportunities. However, Canada replaced those lost to the United States by attracting professionals from Great Britain.

Some Canadians remained in the United States for a relatively short period, but statistics of those who returned are not available. Included among those who returned home were men and women who completed postgraduate work in US universities. In the 1960s, Canadian universities expanded rapidly and several well-educated émigrés returned home to staff these institutions. Highly trained Americans also found academic opportunities north of the border.

POST-WORLD WAR II MEXICAN IMMIGRATION

Unlike Europeans and Cubans, who were the beneficiaries of displaced persons laws and special refugee legislation, Mexicans entered the United States as economic migrants shortly after America's entry into World War II in December 1941. Labor shortages developed in the United States as millions of Americans either headed to war or to cities to work in industries producing goods for the war. Large-scale agricultural producers, who could easily find cheap American laborers during the lean years of the Great Depression, lost workers to these better-paying jobs in war-related factories and shipyards. Thus the agrarian producers turned to the government for help. One source of low-wage labor lay south of the border. Initially, however, many Mexicans and the Mexican government were reluctant to cooperate with the United States. They remembered the repatriation of Mexican nationals and their children during the Great Depression of the 1930s, and they knew how badly Latinos were treated in the United States, especially in Texas, where bigotry flourished.

Ultimately, the opportunity for higher wages overshadowed this reluctance, and beginning in 1942 the United States and Mexico cooperated in a temporary guest worker agreement known as the Bracero Program, which lasted, with short interruptions, until 1964. During its existence the Bracero Program brought nearly five million young Mexicans to the United States to work in agriculture and railroad maintenance. Because many Braceros repeatedly signed on again after their temporary work permits expired, scholars believe that 2.5 million individuals participated in the program. One-half picked crops in California and other states, but some Braceros were employed in a variety of other activities including railroad maintenance. They worked in twenty-one states, mostly in the upper midwestern and western parts of the United States.

During its twenty-two-year history, the Bracero Program provided low-wage labor to mostly agricultural entrepreneurs. The men were supposed to be paid the "prevailing wage," which was forty cents an hour, but with little governmental supervision they received somewhere between thirty and fifty cents per hour. Moreover, even though growers were supposed to provide adequate housing, workers lived under appalling conditions. Investigators found some residing in shacks no better than chicken coops, lacking basic sanitary conditions, and forced

Table 1.3 Braceros Entering the United States Under Contract, 1942–1964

1942	4,203	1950	67,500	1958	432,857
1943	52,098	1951	192,000	1959	437,643
1944	62,170	1952	197,100	1960	315,846
1945	49,454	1953	201,388	1961	291,420
1946	32,043	1954	309,033	1962	194,978
1947	19,632	1955	398,650	1963	186,865
1948	35,345	1956	335,197	1964	177,736
1949	107,000	1957	436,049		

SOURCE: INS, *Annual Reports*, 1942–1965.

to clean themselves with water found in nearby ditches. Under the lax supervision of the Department of Agriculture, growers could be assured that there would be little interference with their mistreatment of these employees.

American businessmen were not the only persons to abuse temporary workers. The Mexican government withheld 10 percent of the Braceros' wages, supposedly to be paid when they completed their employment in the program. But many were not paid; as a result some former Braceros sued the Mexican government for these wages, and in 2005 won their right to receive what was owed to them. But by then many had already died, while most of the surviving Braceros were in their eighties or nineties. Proving they had worked in the United States was not easy, as they did not possess the required paperwork. In 2008 one former Bracero remarked, "All of us Braceros are dead." If a settlement came, he concluded, "It would be for my funeral." Another, unable to produce the necessary documentation, remarked, "I remember everything, the fields, the places, the crops... but they are not accepting my memories."

In spite of the low pay and miserable accommodations, there were still advantages to becoming a Bracero. Wages in the United States were much higher than they were in Mexico. The difference in income made it possible for workers to send remittances home, a practice also common among the European and Asian immigrants since the nineteenth century. As in the past, such remittances allowed relatives to piece together livable lives. During the life of the program Braceros remitted an estimated two hundred million dollars to families back home. Civil rights advocates, labor unions, and other reformers, however, were appalled by the brutal and almost barbaric treatment Braceros received; some were beaten when they failed to perform adequately. Concerned parties pressured the Labor Department and Congress to abolish the program, which the secretary of labor finally did in 1964.

The number of Braceros was limited to totals agreed on by the United States and Mexico, hence many Mexicans, who were unable to become Braceros, crossed into the United States without authorization. If they did not have official papers they were labeled "undocumented" or "illegal aliens." It was relatively easy for

Mexicans to cross the border because the Border Patrol lacked enough agents to cover the nineteen-hundred-mile boundary between the two nations. Once in the United States undocumented Mexicans often labored side by side with Braceros and lived under the same conditions. However, they could be paid less because they were not in the country legally. If caught, they could be deported. Like the Braceros, they were young men with few economic prospects at home.

With the growing number of undocumented immigrants in the late 1940s and early 1950s, officials in Washington, DC, became alarmed and claimed that the border between the nations was too easy to sneak through. The undocumented immigrants were called "illegal aliens" and, often, "wetbacks." The term "wetback" was a reference to the Mexicans who swam or waded across the Rio Grande River to enter the United States. In 1954 President Dwight David Eisenhower directed the Immigration and Naturalization Service (INS) to deport the undocumented immigrants. In a zealous attempt to comply with the president's directive, the INS stopped most of the unauthorized migrants at the border while raiding areas suspected of using men without proper papers. From California to Texas, "Operation Wetback" resulted in over one million individuals being deported that year. . Many farmers cooperated with the government because the INS indicated that in the near future the number of Braceros would increase. Indeed, the Immigration and Naturalization Service agents planted themselves on Texas farms until the owners promised to hire Braceros in the future.

As can be seen in Table 1.3, the number of Braceros increased sharply in the late 1950s. Some undocumented immigrants became Braceros instantaneously when the American government once again allowed the Bracero program to continue. A few commentators offensively tagged this process "drying out the wetbacks." One Texas grower became famous for placing booby traps at his gate to block INS agents. He cursed the officers and lobbied Congress to reduce funds for the Border Patrol. He lost this battle, as the number of illegal workers declined radically, at least for one year. In 1955 the INS apprehended only seventy-eight thousand persons and boasted that "the border was secure." The absurdity of that statement was shown by a rapid increase of undocumented Mexican migrants later in the decade. Although machines were already replacing agricultural laborers by then, increasing production required many hands to work the fields. In 2004 one scholar concluded that the Bracero Program "spawned and institutionalized networks and labor market relationships between Mexico and the United States. These ties continued and became the foundation for today's illegal migration from Mexico."

Legal Mexican immigration also increased during the two decades after World War II, and in some cases the newcomers followed the path of the Braceros. Regular immigrants from Mexico numbered 273,847 in the 1950s, and another 441,824 during the 1960s. These people did not limit their work to agriculture. Instead, they discovered better-paying jobs in expanding urban areas like Houston, Chicago, and Minneapolis. By 1970, 6 percent of Dallas's population was Hispanic; in Chicago, Mexicans constituted the largest number of Hispanics. As a result of such movement, Hispanics in the United States were becoming an urban people and a middle class began to emerge, the product of higher-paying urban jobs and American education. However, most members of the new middle class were second generation.

Urban opportunities also attracted immigrant women. In the post-1945 era more Mexican women than men arrived. Like their male counterparts, they often left families behind and sent remittances to support their kin. Both men and women usually worked in low-wage occupations requiring little skill, only a rudimentary knowledge of English, and little education. For women housework beckoned, as did factory jobs in the Southwest's garment industry

THE MOOD FOR CHANGE

By 1965 it was clear that the national origins quota system was becoming meaningless. Approximately two-thirds of all immigrants were arriving as nonquota. Practically all Western Hemisphere immigrants were nonquota, but roughly one-half of European newcomers bypassed the quota because of special immigration legislation passed between 1945 and 1965. Even the two thousand annual slots allocated to Asia by the McCarran-Walter Immigration Act of 1952 were misleading. Refugees and war brides had swelled the numbers so that Asian nations sent twenty-thousand immigrants to the United States in 1965, ten times the amount prescribed by the 1952 law. Asians amounted to 5 percent of all immigrants in 1965. American legislators who wanted reform believed that the time for change had arrived.

Yet the mood of the nation was not entirely favorable to an altered immigration policy. While liberals generally had their way with the passage of a major new system to select future immigrants, some Americans viewed the rapid increase in Latinos with alarm. Southern whites and residents of rural areas in particular feared an influx of Hispanics as well as Catholics. They wanted growth in the United States to come from Protestants like themselves. To achieve the requisite number of votes for passage of a liberal immigration bill that focused on family unification and filling existing labor needs, authors of the 1965 immigration act used imaginative and compromising solutions.

CHAPTER 2

A New Immigration System

Europeans, West Indians, and the Hart-Celler Act, 1965–1990

Immigration reformers in the 1950s and early 1960s criticized the constant need for special bills to admit refugees, found abhorrent the prejudices written into the McCarran-Walter Act, and thought that American immigration policies should, to some extent, reflect the labor needs of the United States. Moreover, in the midst of the changing social currents of the 1960s, many Americans believed that the new immigration legislation should be nondiscriminatory, reflecting America's highest ideals. On the other hand, many legislators from the South and rural America believed that foreigners from outside of northern and western European communities would pollute American society and undermine its moral and spiritual foundations. Craving cultural conformity, these legislators welcomed the restrictions in existing immigration legislation and opposed a change in the nation's ethnic mix.

While liberal reformers had won some gains with the enactment of the Displaced Persons acts in 1948 and 1950, and the Refugee Relief Act of 1953, they continued to believe that the nation needed a less restrictive immigration policy. As a result of the 1964 elections, liberals held a large majority in Congress and had a forceful president, Lyndon B. Johnson, in the White House who supported their views. Thus, together with some conservatives in Congress, a majority of legislators coalesced to change American immigration law. The new bill, the Immigration Act of 1965, also known as the Hart-Celler Act, created a new system for the Eastern Hemisphere. For that hemisphere ethnic preferences were abolished, family unification was favored, and every nation in the Eastern Hemisphere was limited to a maximum immigration quota of twenty-thousand persons a year, excluding immediate family members (spouses, minor children, and parents of adult US citizens). At the same time the new law also placed a ceiling of 120,000 on the Western Hemisphere.

BACKGROUND FOR CHANGE

There were a number of factors that led to immigration reform in the United States, beginning with the impact of realignment of congressional districts during the 1960s. Until 1962 state legislatures often gerrymandered geographical areas to ensure disproportionate influence for rural residents. For example, a majority of Californians lived in or around Los Angeles, but the city had only 11 percent of the elected members in the state legislature. Rural areas in most states usually included large numbers of native-born Protestant conservatives who abhorred the idea of welcoming Catholic and Jewish immigrants to the United States. But the Supreme Court ruled in *Baker v. Carr* that congressional districts should generally reflect equality of treatment for all citizens, thus state legislatures had to realign political demarcations. As a result of this mandate, the number of members of Congress from urban areas, where most immigrants lived, increased, while thinly populated rural areas' influence declined in the US House of Representatives.

Allowing cities to have more representatives was not the only political change to impact immigration. The new House members and senators reflected the changing social views of the 1960s by passing the civil rights and voting rights acts, trying to eliminate poverty, and increasing federal aid to improve the quality of education in the nation's schools. The 1964 election provided liberal Democrats with a sweeping mandate for change as President Lyndon Johnson, who had succeeded John F. Kennedy after his assassination in November 1963, defeated the more conservative Republican candidate, Senator Barry Goldwater of Arizona in a landslide. Johnson won 61 percent of the popular vote, and all but thirty-nine electoral votes. Johnson's election theme stated that the best way for the American people to honor slain President Kennedy was to pass legislation that he had championed. And with the Democrats capturing a two-thirds majority in both the House of Representatives and the Senate, Johnson seized the opportunity to persuade and pressure Congress to enact many liberal reforms, including Medicare, which provided medical care to senior citizens; Medicaid, which provided medical care to the poor; and Head Start, a program to help poor children prepare for kindergarten.

In addition to these reforms, legislators also focused on revising existing immigration statutes. Foreign affairs, which had played such a large role in the formation of immigration policy during the developing Cold War, was still important for reformers. Along with the legacy of World War II, refugee problems also affected senior government officials' thoughts on immigration policy. The administration sent Secretary of State Dean Rusk to Congress to discuss how existing national origins restrictions hurt American relations with Asian and European nations. Rusk, a native of Georgia, was not the ideal messenger since he believed that "we are an Anglo-Saxon country" and should remain so. However, he served at the pleasure of the president and did as he was told. While testifying before a congressional committee, the secretary of state made a strong case for eliminating the restrictive and discriminatory national origins immigration policy that affected how foreign nations viewed the United States.

Ethnic lobbying of Congress also played a role. In the 1920s and 1930s groups friendly to immigrants had little influence with members of Congress. But during the early 1960s proimmigration organizations became more focused and forceful in advocating the end of national origins quotas. They replaced the more traditional patriotic groups, such as the Daughters of the American Revolution and the American Legion, in shaping immigration policy.

A final roadblock to reform had ended with the deaths of Senator Patrick McCarran in 1954 and Congressman Francis Walter in 1963. The removal of these two congressional leaders, both conservative Democrats, was crucial, and their influence and committee chairmanships were replaced by the liberal authors of the Immigration Act of 1965, Representative Emanuel Celler (D, NY) and Senator Philip Hart (D, MI).

THE HART-CELLER ACT

Both presidents Harry Truman and Dwight Eisenhower had been critical of the national origins system and had made suggestions for reform, although neither president recommended abolishing quotas. President Kennedy went a step further, writing a book, *A Nation of Immigrants*, detailing how immigrants had contributed to the growth and accomplishments of the United States. He called for the abolition of the national origins system. Although Lyndon Johnson, as a senator from Texas, had supported the McCarran-Walter Act in 1952, as president he was anxious to show that he would follow Kennedy's lead.

The Hart-Celler Act reflected liberals' views. National origins as a concept was abolished; in its stead family unification prevailed for the Eastern Hemisphere. Congressman Michael Feighan (D, OH), who chaired the subcommittee on immigration, had a great influence on the final product. He favored a provision in the new act that would give preference to family members of American citizens and resident aliens. This preference could be supported by conservatives as well as liberals because it was assumed that the patterns of post-1945 immigration would remain the same. True, the new law would facilitate immigration from southern Europe, but the special laws passed after 1945 had already brought many people from that area to the United States. As Congressman Emanuel Celler told his colleagues in the House of Representatives, "Since the people of Africa and Asia have very few relatives here, comparatively few could immigrate [to the United States] from those countries." Even the American Legion, one of those patriotic groups with little voice in the debates, agreed that there would be little change in the origins of future immigrants. Few, if any, legislators, or other Americans, understood how the family unification provision could lead to a different kind of ethnic mix in the future.

The Immigration Act became effective in 1968 and allowed a total of 170,000 immigrants from the Eastern Hemisphere to enter the United States in any one year, which was slightly more than under the current policy, with a maximum of twenty-thousand for each nation, excluding immediate family members of United States citizens, who entered over quotas. Most visas were to be granted to persons with close relatives of immigrants and citizens living in the United States.

But opponents of radical changes also won a point. As noted above, the law also created a ceiling of 120,000 for people from the Western Hemisphere but without a preference system and national limit. The Johnson administration had not wanted a ceiling for the Western Hemisphere, but it gave into conservatives' insistence upon limiting immigration from the Western Hemisphere.

From 1945 to 1965 immigration from the Western Hemisphere had averaged 110,000 per annum, but large increases in the early 1960s alarmed those in Congress who wanted to limit future growth of Hispanics, especially Mexicans and Central Americans. Congress established a special commission to review the impact on the new legislation on peoples from the Western Hemisphere. The commission let it be known when it reported in 1968 that it was concerned about an influx of Hispanics not Canadians. The Western Hemisphere did not receive a preference system and national limit until 1976. In 1978 Congress combined the two hemispheres to create a world wide system with preferences and a national limit of 20,000 and a total of 290,000 immigrants, excluding immediate family members of US citizens.

As noted, under the new system immediate family members of US citizens could enter without being counted against existing quotas. When the Hart-Celler Act had been written in 1965 this exemption was thought to be a minor one; in time, however, the numbers mushroomed, and family members of immigrants became the largest category of foreigners admitted to the country.

When President Johnson signed the Immigration Act of 1965 at the Statue of Liberty in October 1965, he reiterated the sentiments expressed previously by Congressman Celler and the American Legion. "This is not a revolutionary bill," he observed. "It does not affect the lives of millions. It will not reshape the structure of our daily lives, or add importantly to our wealth and power....It repairs a deep and painful flaw in the fabric of American justice." At first Johnson's prediction was accurate. During the first decade of the law's existence Europeans dominated immigrant numbers to the United States.

ITALIANS, GREEKS AND PORTUGUESE

Italians made the largest numerical gains from the Immigration Act of 1965. Eager to leave home because their economy, the newcomers who entered the United States after 1945 differed from previous immigrant groups from Italy, arriving as

Table 2.1 The Hart-Celler Act as Amended in 1978

1st Preference	Unmarried adult children of US citizens	20%
2nd Preference	Spouses and children of permanent resident aliens	20%
3rd Preference	Members of professions and scientists of exceptional ability	10%
4th Preference	Married children of US citizens	10%
5th Preference	Brothers and Sisters of US citizens	24%
6th Preference	Skilled and unskilled workers in occupations for which labor is in short supply	10%
7th Preference	Refugees from communist dominated countries or the Middle East	6%

Table 2.2 Immigrants to the United States from Selected European
Nations

	1945–1965	1965–1984
Ireland	115,813	36,188
Germany	548,590	186,368
Greece	73,110	180,844
Italy	318,487	279,576
Portugal	38,128	188,643

SOURCE: Office of Statistics, US Department of Homeland Security, *Statistical Yearbook*, 2008.

family members of Americans, being better educated and possessing higher levels of skills than previously arriving countrymen. About one-third of the post–World War II Italian immigrants settled in the New York City area, while the others spread out to numerous communities across the United States. Many of the Italians who arrived were aided in their adjustment by friends and relatives as well as private and public agencies that offered them linguistic aid. If they spoke English, it facilitated their acculturation to American society. So too did the economic and social benefits that they derived from being with other family members. Historian Donna Gabaccia described the new and highly skilled Italian immigrants as "more secular in orientation, urban in origin, and left-wing in their politics.... [They] are more comfortable with cosmopolitan identities as Italians and Europeans."

Greeks also benefited greatly from the Hart-Celler Act, showing the largest percentage increases as a result of this legislation. Before 1965 Greeks had a quota of only 307 persons per year and had to depend heavily on the special bills enacted during the postwar era to gain extra visas for entry. As a result of the Hart-Celler Act, however, over one hundred thousand Greeks, mostly using the family preferences, arrived in the 1970s, marking the largest increase in any ten-year period. To a large degree the Greek exodus was motivated by a depressed economy at home after the end of World War II, with Greece's economic revival in the late 1970s reducing the numbers of emigrants.

It is likely that the civil war from 1946 to 1949 and the military dictatorship from 1967 to 1974 contributed to emigration, particularly for some highly educated professionals. Greek immigration tallies were augmented by sailors who illegally abandoned their ships in American ports. Between 1957 and 1974 several thousand of these men dispersed throughout the United States, the largest number of sailors from any nationality to enter the United States in this fashion.

Greeks who came to the United States settled in both urban and suburban areas, with the largest number choosing to reside in New York State. Other Greeks found new homes in California, Illinois, Massachusetts, New Jersey, Pennsylvania, and Ohio. By 1990, Astoria, a section in the borough of Queens, contained the largest Greek immigrant community in United States. Public elementary schools in the area were attuned to the children's needs and developed a bilingual Greek-English curriculum.

Like Italians, Greeks maintain strong family consciousness, embracing traditional values and a fairly conservative outlook, but not rigidly so. Their communities are rooted in the Greek Orthodox Church, which supports language and cultural programs for children and adults alike. Modern Greek men are expected to be responsible husbands and fathers, and both parents sacrifice to ensure their children's success. Boys are guided toward study and strongly encouraged to prepare for careers in prestigious positions in law, medicine, and engineering as adults. In the past Greek girls and women were carefully sheltered, but younger Greek adults have accommodated themselves to contemporary American values and culture.

Like so many Greeks in the past, post-1965 newcomers opened small food businesses, such as groceries, vegetable markets, coffee shops, pizza parlors, and fine restaurants. By the late 1970s, Greeks were the largest group of coffee shop and diner owners in New York City. In 1966 Chicago had only one Greek restaurant but in 1978 there were twenty in the city. Greeks also became tailors, shoe repairmen, and taxicab drivers—especially in New York City.

Many second-generation Greeks were well aware of the long hours required in occupations and running small family enterprisers. Thus while the immigrant generation worked long hours, they encouraged their children to seek opportunities in the professions. In the second generation over half of Greek men, and many Greek women, occupied professional, managerial, sales, administrative, and technical jobs.

AN IMMIGRANT'S TALE

Nick Karkambasis came to America, arriving on December 22, 1969. He did what so many other Greeks did. He was employed in his uncle's Delta Diner on Long Island, New York. After working as a busboy, cook, and dishwasher, he bought his own diner in 1988. Other Greeks like him opened many coffee shops in New York City, while in Connecticut, Greek immigrants opened or purchased pizza parlors.

He worked long hours and supervised his staff and food carefully. Such attention eventually paid off, and his diner prospered. However, his two children, who graduated from college, had no desire to follow their father into the diner business. He even had difficulty recruiting staff, as Greek immigration to the United States slowed in the late 1970s. Karkambasis then hired South Americans. Karkambasis knew that his children would not follow him. They simply did not want to work as hard, noted Karkambasis. As Karkambasis pondered retirement, so did several hundred other Greeks who owned diners in the New York area. But who would replace them? The answer was found in new Asian immigrants who were looking to open small business to achieve their dreams in America.

Portugal, the third European nation to benefit most from the Immigration Act of 1965, was neutral in World War II and hence had not experienced the damage so prevalent in Italy, Russia, and Poland. But Portugal was the poorest nation in Western Europe. Moreover, from the 1930s to 1974 it was ruled by a dictator, Antonio Salazar, who did little to promote economic growth. The Portuguese under Salazar found themselves engaged in war in Angola, Mozambique, and the Cape Verde Islands, fighting to keep these nations as Portuguese colonies. Finally, the army revolted, enabling the former colonies to gain independence in the 1970s. Moreover, the rebels created a new democratic Portugal. But the nation had been drained economically in its struggles with former colonists, and these battles resulted in many Portuguese seeking opportunities elsewhere, including the United States. However, the Portugal quota was only 440 under previous national origins legislation, meaning that those who came before Hart-Celler needed special laws to supplement their totals.

From 1965 to 1980 over 120,000 Portuguese, 80 percent of whom originated in the Azores, immigrated to the United States. The newcomers headed to eastern Massachusetts, Rhode Island, and California, where thousands of their fellow countrymen had already settled. Newark, New Jersey, housed the largest single Portuguese community in the United States, while another significant group joined communities in and around Santa Clara, California.

The sluggish Portuguese economy prompted professionals and businessmen to abandon their country for greater opportunities elsewhere, but villagers with minimal skills also proved eager to leave. When Portuguese Americans later visited their homeland they spoke of American riches, enormous comforts, and vast opportunities awaiting enterprising individuals. The existence of cheap air fares to the United States also served as an inducement for the Portuguese to seek their fortunes in America. Like so many immigrants before them, Portuguese migrants looked back with nostalgia. One young woman on the eve of her departure remarked,

> It was summer.... I looked at the blue sky and its cotton balls of clouds, I gazed at the green fields that extended beyond the horizon, and I was sad. In a few hours, I would be far away, far from the land of my birth.... In a few hours I would leave for the Promised Land with a heavy heart and tears in my eyes.

The United States was not the only nation to receive Greeks, Italians, and Portuguese. Australia, Canada, and several South American nations liberalized their immigration laws in the late 1940s and 1950s to permit southern Europeans and Asians to enter. For example, in its 2006 census Australia reported roughly two hundred thousand persons of Italian birth.

GERMAN NEWCOMERS

While the Immigration Act of 1965 Act helped Italians, Greeks, and Portuguese, it had little impact on Germans. By that time the harsh economic conditions of postwar Germany had ended. The "miracle economy" of West Germany had absorbed most of its internal refugees as well as the *Volksdeutsche* (ethnic Germans who had been expelled from Eastern European countries at the end of World War II) and those left homeless because of the war. The booming industrial progress not only absorbed the expellees and discouraged Germans from emigrating, but it necessitated the importation of foreign labor.

As a result, Germany and France, two of the more productive countries, recruited employees in other parts of Europe including Italy, Greece, Portugal, and Turkey, the largest supplier of unskilled labor. By the 1970s there was no longer a labor shortage in the north, but Germany had already taken in over six hundred thousand Italians and untold numbers of Turks. Within a few years the southern European nations were themselves prospering, fewer of their citizens emigrated, and they needed additional workers from other countries. Both Africans and Asians arrived to fill the abundant and new employment slots throughout Europe. As a result of these population movements many European nations became multicultural without thinking ahead about how the newcomers might complicate, and add to, social unrest.

Moreover, Germans from the communist east still managed to cross into West Germany in spite of the barriers separating the two German nations. A few thousand easterners eventually migrated to America. Some skilled West Germans also immigrated to America after 1968, alarming German officials because so many of these émigrés were well educated and possessed exceptional skills. Thomas Bauer, a labor economist, explained that in Germany, in contrast to other Western European nations, a hostile economic climate punished highly skilled persons. "The taxes are too high," he wrote, "the wages are too low and feelings of jealousy towards high-income earners are widespread. This is a special deterrent to the highly qualified."

The number of German immigrants reaching the United States decreased from 209,616 in the 1960s to 85,752 in the 1980s. Additional German tourists, students, and temporary workers obtained visas for America, although most of these persons had no intention of remaining for extended periods. In the 1990s, however, over half of Germans, French, and other Europeans receiving Ph.D.s in American universities remained in the United States permanently, but the numbers were only a few thousand yearly. One notable change among this post–World War II German cadre was that women exceeded men among the new arrivals, which was the pattern for most post-1945 immigrants, although in some years males were a majority. In part, war brides explain the slight majority of women, but family unification also contributed to the movement of women, as did a changing social atmosphere that allowed women much more independence than they had before World War II.

NEW IMMIGRANTS FROM THE UNITED KINGDOM

With the passage of the Immigration Act of 1965, the United Kingdom lost the privileged spot it had obtained from the American quota system since the

Table 2.3 British Immigrants by Major Occupational Group

	1950	1960	1970
Professional, technical, and kindred workers	1,215	3,187	1,781
Managers, administrators, and proprietors	582	642	574
Craftsmen, foremen, and kindred workers	1,465	1,949	496

SOURCE: INS, *Annual Reports, 1950–1970.*

1920s; however, this made little impact in British emigration to the United States. Newcomers from the United Kingdom averaged about twenty-two thousand a year in the 1960s, and fewer people came in subsequent decades. In 2009 only 15,748 people arrived from the United Kingdom. The above figures indicate how the little the Hart-Celler Act influenced the exodus of well-educated and highly trained individuals.

With the improved British economy of the 1980s, fewer of the highly educated citizens sought fulfillment of their dreams in the United States. Yet a steady number still migrated because, as one immigrant put it, "America has always been known as the land of opportunity. I came to see if it's true."

THE NEW IRISH

The Immigration Act of 1965 actually curtailed Irish emigration to America. Before 1968, the year the Hart-Celler Act went into effect, one commentator noted, "pretty much any Irish man or woman who wanted to immigrate could just pick up and do so, with relative ease"; between 1945 and 1967 nearly one hundred thousand people departed the Emerald Isle for America. The departure from Eire reflected the diffuse performance of the Irish economy, and not until economic conditions improved did the exodus subside. In the early 1970s, however, the Irish economy soured again, prompting many young adults to look for opportunities across the Atlantic Ocean. But the rules specified in the new legislation curtailed their options. In the 1970s only 11,641 Irish immigrants came to America. Semiskilled and unskilled men and women lacked the close relatives in the United States necessary to use family unification, while their limited vocational accomplishments prevented them from applying for occupational visas. As a result, many young Irish men and women traveled to Great Britain or to the United States as visitors, overstayed their visa expiration date, and thus became undocumented immigrants.

The "New Irish" without legal status settled mostly in Boston, New York, and Chicago. No accurate figures exist as to their numbers, but by the 1980s estimates ranged between 44,000 and 136,000 people. Living in existing Irish-American communities, they formed cultural networks. The well-educated blended into American society and obtained positions suitable to their backgrounds. The less well educated men found work in construction, while the women worked in traditional occupations: child care, house cleaning, and waitressing. They faced no discrimination from the people around them and the newcomers made no effort to hide from authorities. They even flaunted themselves in public. One of the people who arrived in the Boston area early in the decade stated, "I don't feel that I'm doing anything illegal. I'm trying to make a future for myself."

The rallying cry for the undocumented newcomers was "Legalize the Irish." Most other Americans did not regard the Irish as unwelcome minorities and were sympathetic to their plight. The Irish Immigration Reform Movement started up to help these undocumented immigrants, as did a new newspaper, the *Irish Voice*. In its first issue the *Irish Voice* editorialized, "This newspaper will be forthright in its attempts to win the estimated 135,000 Irish illegals their proper places as full members of society."

By the 1980s the Irish were not the only unauthorized immigrants in the United States; they were joined by Poles, Filipinos, and Mexicans, among others. American voters of different ethnic heritages urged Congress to legislate a solution to the problem of illegal aliens in this country. In response, Congress passed the 1986 Immigration Reform and Control Act. A small section of the law established a one-time lottery for ten thousand immigrant visas; Irish communities in both America and Ireland were particularly aware of the new opportunity. Immigration offices were flooded with hundreds of thousands of applications from the Irish, who then won about forty percent of the available places.

Despite the 1986 law, Congress remained under pressure to provide further opportunities for Irish and other Europeans who sought entry into the country. The Dublin government also urged its Washington embassy to lobby for favorable émigré legislation. Boston's Tip O'Neill, speaker of the US House of Representatives, successfully used his influence to push for the desired bill. The Immigration Act of 1990 again increased the number of slots available for legal immigrants. One of the bill's provisions established another immigrant lottery for forty thousand diversity visas (DVs) designed for people "adversely affected" by the Hart-Celler Act of 1965. Under this act the Irish were to receive forty percent of the DVs for the first three years. After the bill passed *The New York Times* editorialized, "It was pretty much all that the Irish had hoped for.... [It provided] virtual amnesty to all the illegal Irish in the country." After the initial three years the Irish lost their legal advantage, but they no longer needed the lottery because the Irish economy revived in the early 1990s, and Irish immigration to the United States averaged only two thousand persons yearly in the 2000s. After 2008 the Irish economy crashed and once again prompted Irish men and women to seek their fortunes elsewhere. Many went to Canada and Australia, but some also headed for the United States again.

SOVIET JEWS AND POLISH IMMIGRANTS

Europeans living under communism did not benefit from the Hart-Celler Act because the existing communist governments did not want people leaving their countries, especially those with skills. However, when Czech students and moderate communist leaders called for a relaxation of communism in the spring of 1968, the hard-line leaders and the Soviet Union quickly crushed the revolt. Several thousand Czechs emigrated and were eventually granted refugee status in the United States. Romania was another source for discontent, and thousands of Romanians left home and a few went to the United States.

Agitation in the United States in the 1970s for the Soviet government to release Jews who wanted to emigrate resulted in Congress withdrawing favorable trade status until the Soviet Union relented. The pressure worked temporarily. Many of the Jews who left went to the United States, where immigration and welfare organizations, such as the New York Association for New Americans (NYANA) and the Hebrew Immigrant Aid Society (HIAS), helped the newcomers adjust to new lives in the United States.

There were several reasons for Jews to emigrate from the Soviet Union. First, the years of living under the brutal dictatorship of Joseph Stalin,who ruled from 1924 to 1953, had taken their toll with the many hardships forcing Russians,

AN IMMIGRANT'S TALE

Irene and Andrej Bozek and their family wanted to leave Poland and settle in the United States. In the spring of 1974 Andrej took his son on a legal vacation to Austria, leaving behind Irene and their two other children. While in Austria he applied for and was granted political asylum in the United States, which was entirely unexpected. The American government liked to grant asylum to persons from communist nations to demonstrate what freedom meant in the West. Irene was informed that, because her husband had participated in a documentary film that was critical of Poland, the Polish government would not allow her and their two children to leave. It was common practice for the communist nations to permit only part of a family to leave, even temporarily.

Irene knew nothing about the film. She "was mad" that her husband seemed to have doomed their prospects for family reunification in America. Then the Polish government reversed its rejection and granted Irene permission to join her husband in the United States. The government gave no reason for its switch in position. When she received asylum in 1975 she joined her husband in New York City. Eventually the couple settled in Texas, where they secured employment and purchased a home. Irene worked for a bookbinder in Austin, where they raised their three children. Their story was especially notable since they knew very little English while in Poland. The family members became the central figures of a CBS documentary film called *To America*.

including Jews, to go without basic necessities. Moreover, anti-Semitism was a constant factor in Soviet life, and it became fierce at times. During the 1980s the government did little to halt the spread of anti-Semitism and actually fostered it. As a result, thousands of Soviet Jews sought opportunities to escape their harsh living conditions. Most would have to wait for the end of the Cold War before emigrating.

As a group, Poles constituted the largest number of migrants from a European communist nation between 1965 and 1989. The Polish government rejected many requests from citizens wishing to emigrate, even though it provided more exit visas than its neighbors did. The United States government permitted some of the visitors to receive asylum and become immigrants, but the largest number benefited after September 1980, when an independent trade union, Solidarity, was organized by Polish workers at the Gdansk Shipyard. The communist government strongly opposed the demands of this labor group for greater freedom and control over their own lives but was finally forced to negotiate with the organization. The turmoil lasted for a decade. During the 1980s the American government was unwilling to deport thousands of Polish visitors in the United States when their temporary visas expired, granting them refugee status instead.

WEST INDIANS

The Hart-Celler Act put all the nations of the Eastern Hemisphere on an equal basis, and each one had the possibility of sending as many as twenty-thousand people annually to the United States. It had not been Congress's intention to bring large numbers of non-Caucasians to the United States. Yet the experience of immigrants from two nations, Jamaica, and Trinidad and Tobago, proved how complicated the issue could be. Traditionally West Indians had migrated to other places in the Caribbean to find work. When the Panama Canal was being built in the first decade of the twentieth century, West Indians found employment there. When the canal was complete, they went with their "Panama Money" to New York City. There was no quota to prevent them from immigrating to the United States, and even after the quota acts of the 1920s were passed, West Indians living in British colonies could migrate under the large British quota. However, under the McCarran-Walter Act of 1952, Jamaica, and Trinidad and Tobago had been given quotas of one hundred persons per year, quotas that remained even after those two colonies became independent. In 1963 only 210 quota immigrants were recorded from Jamaica. Certain close relatives of US citizens were permitted to enter over the quota, but even then the total for Jamaica was less than two thousand. As a result of the limitations that the United States had placed on West Indians, a growing number of them headed to Great Britain. With the passage of the McCarran-Walter Act of 1952, the number of West Indians immigrating to Great Britain exploded. England became increasingly alarmed by this event and, as a result, enacted legislation in 1962 to curb further entry of Indians, Pakistanis, and West Indians.

In the early 1960s, American officials recognized that while most people in the Western Hemisphere could enter the United States without quota restrictions, an inequity existed for Jamaica, and Trinidad and Tobago. Administration officials told Congress that ending the one hundred–limit quota on West Indians would open the door for peoples of former British colonies in the Caribbean. Yet officials did not anticipate the entry of significant numbers of West Indians. Within a few years after the Immigration Act of 1965 went into effect, however, Jamaican immigration had reached ten thousand annually, and émigrés showed no inclination to curtail their movement. During the 1980s, 193,874 West Indians migrated to the United States. People from other Caribbean nations, like Haiti and the Dominican Republic also joined the movement north to the United States. The largest collection of West Indians gravitated to New York City, where, in 2012, black immigrants comprised over one-quarter of the city's African American population.

West Indians had a reputation for hard work and political participation. Certainly in New York City they already had a history of political involvement because some of the city's first black leaders hailed from Caribbean nations. West Indians were also known to be entrepreneurs, and about 10 percent ran their own businesses, a figure that approximated the national average for self-employment. For the most part West Indians, especially after the opening of positions due to the civil rights movement, preferred white-collar occupations and careers in health care.

Among the first West Indians to immigrate under the Hart-Celler Act were women, who could qualify with occupational visas as nannies or domestics. These young women easily found positions, but after several years many of them moved on to higher paying employment. In the meantime, they sent money home to their families and later, when they became citizens, sponsored their relatives under the family preferences provisions of the 1965 immigration act.

The better educated West Indians found well-paying opportunities outside of New York City; even southern states that black immigrants had avoided before the civil rights movement of the 1960s provided opportunities for them. Because of their relatively good education, and ability to speak English, Jamaicans and other Anglophones found employment as teachers, nurses, and other health care workers. After New York City, Washington, DC, housed the largest number of West Indians. Observers believed that these Caribbean immigrants were originally drawn to the nation's capital because of Howard University, perhaps the leading African American institution of higher learning in the United States. Some West Indians did, in fact, arrive in this country as students, received their education at Howard, and then applied for immigrant status. The nation's capital also provided the opportunity for West Indians to find employment in foreign embassies.

A high proportion of West Indian men and women were well educated and therefore earned more money than immigrants who were not so well trained. Moreover, they had low divorce rates, and consequently their households were not likely to be female-headed. The fact that a majority of black students at Harvard University in the 2000s were the children of West Indians and Africans added to the belief in the "success" story of West Indians. Despite their abilities and achievements, West Indian earnings do not match those of whites with comparable education and skills.

Black immigrants, whether from Africa or the Caribbean, encountered American urban racial segregation when they sought housing accommodations. This meant that many of them were forced to live in areas where crime rates were high, drugs were easily available, and schools were overcrowded and underserviced. In fact, a few families have sent their children back to their homelands for schooling, and some African immigrants opened special schools for their children in the United States.

In retrospect it appears that Congress expected Southern and Eastern Europeans to benefit most from passage of the Hart-Celler Act. Through the late 1970s that was largely true. The legislators had not foreseen that hundreds of thousands of West Indians would also be given much greater opportunities to immigrate. They knew that some increases would occur for Asians and Near Easterners, but they certainly did not anticipate that millions would arrive. They also failed to consider the rapid growth of the Asian populations in India, China, and Pakistan, nor the creation of new nations occurring after the collapse of European colonies, which then became eligible for an immigration quota of twenty thousand. Because relatively few Asians, and even fewer Africans, had arrived as immigrants in the United States before 1965, aside from war brides and refugees, Congress did not anticipate that these people would make much of a dent in the numbers of newcomers and did not believe that their numbers would increase substantially. Within a decade lawmakers realized that family unification provisions allowed all citizens to sponsor their close relatives from abroad. Legislators had not anticipated the large numbers of new citizens who would take advantage of this opportunity. Nor did they realize the impact that this chain migration would have.

CHAPTER 3

The Hart-Celler Act and Immigrants from Asia and the Middle East, 1965–1990

When Congress passed the Hart-Celler Act in 1965, most Americans favored maintaining the existing American ethnic composition. But the composition would change dramatically during the 1970s and 1980s, when large numbers of Asians arrived. While not anticipating this migration, Congress did nothing to stop it. Immigration legislation had been on the back burner during most of the 1950s, but, as noted, in 1964 liberal Democrats more sympathetic to broadening and rationalizing American immigration policies won overwhelming victories in the November elections. Combined with a change in leadership in the House and Senate immigration subcommittees and a forceful president anxious for new legislation on the subject, Congress seriously worked on revising existing laws. Table 3.1 indicates the dramatic shift in immigration patterns.

BACKGROUND

A reporter for *Science* magazine provided one clue in 1968 as to why so many Asians entered America between 1965 and 1990. "A handful of American officials," he wrote, "have been aware for several months that a dramatic shift in the composition of the brain drain was likely, but this realization did not reach a wider public until the State Department's Visa Office published a detailed analysis of

Table 3.1 Immigration from Europe and Asia

	EUROPE	ASIA
1950s	1,404,973	135,844
1960s	1,133,443	358,605
1970s	825,590	1,406,544
1980s	668,866	2,859,899

SOURCE: US Department of Homeland Security (DHS), *Statistical Yearbook*, 2008.

the new law late in November." The writer referred to the fact that many Asians were obtaining immigrant visas as professional workers. The change in the law occurred just when large numbers of British, German, and Canadian professionals were no longer eager to settle in the United States.

Yet even a decline in European professionals and skilled workers does not fully explain the shift, because professionals were allocated only a small quota in the Hart-Celler legislation. Asian professionals if they naturalized years later, could sponsor their brothers and sisters under the preference system. Even more important, US citizens could sponsor immediate family members from abroad without regard for quotas. The provision for immediate family members became increasingly important, and by the 2000s over four hundred thousand persons yearly were benefiting from it. Asians, who had high rates of naturalization, were keenly aware of the importance of what was called chain migration, the sponsoring of families to follow the original immigrant.

Another important post-1945 factor for immigration was the decolonization of former colonies by the United States, Japan, and Europe. As former colonies gained independence they became eligible for the national quotas of twenty thousand. Later on, the 1990 Immigration Act gave national quotas of twenty thousand the flexibility to increase, and by 2009 the annual quota reached 25,620.

Post-1945 migration to the United States was part of a global movement of peoples other than Asians. While immigration from Europe had been declining since the 1970s, it did not completely dry up. Following the end of the Cold War in 1989, many East Europeans who had lived under communism headed west. And Latin Americans were also on the move.

TAIWANESE

In 1949 the communists won control of mainland China, and followers of the defeated nationalist government who could afford to do so moved to the island of Taiwan or to British-controlled Hong Kong. About three to four million members of the nationalist army along with the wealthy and small-businesspeople made up the bulk of these two groups. The United States favored the nationalists over the communists. Some of the provisions of the McCarran-Walter Act as well as minor legislative acts in the 1950s made it possible for a few thousand Chinese to get to America.

The lure was the American system of higher education. American universities had emerged after World War II as the best in the world. In Taiwan many families made sure that their children learned English so that they might enter universities in the United States. From 1949 to 1990 over one hundred thousand Taiwanese studied in the United States. Some of the graduates found jobs that qualified them to remain in America. In the 1960s, fewer than 16,000 Taiwanese immigrants were recorded, but in the 1970s the figure topped 83,000, and 119,051 arrived in the following decade when nearly one-third of all Taiwanese Americans reached the United States. As economic opportunities increased at home fewer

Photo 3-1   A Touch of Taiwan in New York City

Taiwanese emigrated. Moreover, some of the Taiwanese students who had benefited from an American education returned to their homeland in the late 1980s and after. Martial law, which had been established in Taiwan, ended in 1987, the island enjoyed a higher standard of living, and the new government established special research centers to entice their well-educated émigrés to return home.

For several decades after passage of the Immigration Act of 1965 almost all Chinese immigrants to the United States arrived from Hong Kong and Taiwan. Great Britain controlled the Hong Kong peninsula and permitted residents to emigrate. Ninety percent of those who immigrated to the United States from these two areas headed to existing urban Chinese American enclaves. A majority of these Chinese American communities had been established in the western part of the United States during the second half of the nineteenth century. As a result, the newest wave of Chinese migrants settled among people whose customs were already familiar. California, Washington, and Oregon Asian communities saw their populations swell, and Las Vegas, Nevada, which had received few Chinese migrants in earlier decades, developed its own Chinatown. New York City's Chinese immigrant population also mushroomed in the last third of the twentieth century. Some of the Chinese newcomers ventured to the southern states, where they joined other non-Chinese Asians. By the 1980s, 20 percent of all Asian immigrants settled in the American South, an area that had received only a handful of Asians before World War II. A good number of these Asians were attracted to jobs requiring education in scientific fields.

MOTHER'S DAY 효도세일
(일부품목 제외)
20%
행사기간 : 5월 1일 - 5월 9일

Photo 3-2 Mothers' Day, Asian Style

Many of the post-1965 Asian immigrants who were financially secure headed for the suburbs. Monterey Park, California, was alleged to have been the nation's first suburb where immigrants from Taiwan, Hong Kong, and the People's Republic of China became the dominant groups in the community. The Taiwanese growth began when a Chinese American developer placed ads for available property in Monterey Park in Hong Kong and Taiwanese newspapers. While Monterey Park became known as "Little Taipei," in reality the majority who lived in the area were not from Taiwan, although they were ethnic Chinese.

Elsewhere, New York City housed the largest single Chinese community in the nation, and the onrush of more immigrants overwhelmed the city's well-established Chinatown. As a result, housing became more costly there and thousands of newcomers developed smaller Chinatowns in the outer boroughs. The Flushing section of Queens was estimated to have one of the largest enclaves of Chinese in America and was especially attractive for the Taiwanese.

Many immigrants from Taiwan and Hong Kong arrived in America without marketable skills. Fortunately, coming with other family members helped ease their adjustment in the United States. So too did strong family values, religious commitments, and a determination to educate their children. These factors often made menial work in factories and restaurants tolerable for the older generation. One did not have to speak English to perform simple, repetitive tasks on assembly lines or peel potatoes and carrots in restaurant kitchens. And jobs were plentiful, for there was scarcely a city or suburb in the United States that did not have at least one Chinese restaurant that needed low-skilled employees.

Unlike the Chinese immigrants of the nineteenth century, many of the newer immigrants had been well educated at home and did not have to succumb to low wage employment. Many of them settled in California's Silicon Valley, which became known as the computer center of America. Other newcomers were experienced entrepreneurs who established small businesses. A few invested in real estate. Not until the late 1980s, after the communist Chinese government lifted rigid controls on emigration, did large numbers arrive from mainland China.

SOUTH KOREANS

Most Americans first became aware of Korea in late June 1950, when the Korean War (1950–1953) began. But South Korea did not receive a quota of twenty thousand until 1965. As a result in 1970 fewer than thirty-five thousand South Koreans lived in the United States. From 1970 until 2010 more than a million of them arrived. The government of North Korea did not permit its people to emigrate. The peak decade for Korean immigration was the 1980s. Although people came from various walks of life in Korea, over 30 percent had a bachelor's degree or higher, while a significant number were well-educated urban professionals; many of the newer arrivals were physicians, nurses, and pharmacists. American-style medical schools had been established in Korea long before 1965. Modern medical practices impressed Korean doctors, who then became eager to go to America. In addition, Koreans learned of American culture through television and the presence of American troops.

The wreckage of the Korean War was also a major factor in Korean immigration. That war took one million lives, as South Korean cities and countryside experienced battles, bombing, and bloodshed. It took several decades for the Korean economy to recover; not until after the 1980s did South Korea become a major player in the economy of Asia. Moreover, from 1965 to 1997 South Korea was run by military dictatorships. In 1976 a journalist published a series of articles on migration to the United States, which presented a harsh view of immigrant life in America. As a book, however, *Day and Night of Komericans: A Visit to Korea in the United States* became a guide to immigration. Those who spoke English fared well in the United States. Those who lacked English-language skills had problems passing licensing requirements and sought economic opportunities outside of the fields in which they had been trained. For the most part, Koreans either joined or established communities in Los Angeles, New York, Chicago, and Washington, DC.

For Korean immigrants it was important to have stability and security, which they often obtained by running their own businesses. At least 20 percent of Koreans, or more than double the rate of members of other immigrant groups or Americans generally, owned their own businesses. Some of their college graduates may not have spoken English well but they ran enterprises successfully. Both men and women were important in the formation and management of family

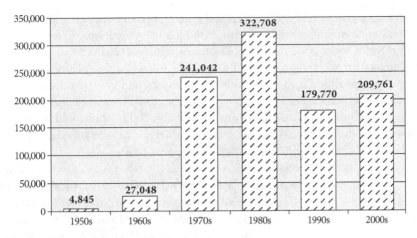

Figure 3.1 Korean Immigration by Decade
SOURCE: DHS, *Statistical Yearbook*, 2010.

Photo 3-3 Two Cultures: Korean Toast Combined with Italian Gelato

endeavors, but sometimes the women were not reported as workers. Husbands and wives labored long hours, and children often helped out when they were not in school. Moreover, Korean stores often employed many of the owners' relatives.

One of the first businesses that post-1965 Korean immigrants obtained were small-scale fruit and vegetable shops being sold by previous generations of Jewish

and Italian owners because their sons and daughters sought opportunities in professional endeavors. *Time* magazine reported the tale of one Korean green grocer
in New York City in 1985. Young Jun Kwon began his workday at 2 a.m. He went to
the wholesale market to purchase fruits and vegetables before opening the family
store. Then his wife, Ok Kyung, and brother cleaned and prepared the fruits and
vegetables for their customers before opening the store for twelve hours every day
of the week. Young Kwon recalled long work hours, "I thought I could go on with
three or four hours of sleep forever, but it seems that I can't any more. I've tried,
but I can't." He made it through the day with several catnaps.

Korean small businesses were scattered alongside those of several other
ethnic groups. Some areas, such as Palisades Park, New Jersey, with its dozens
of Korean-run stores, could be labeled ethnic ghettos, but those were the excep-
tion. Los Angeles's "Korea Town" was one place where members of several ethnic
groups ran stores. Some women established beauty parlors, but by 1990 they had
to compete with shops run by Vietnamese immigrants. As one Korean quipped,
"Just how many nail salons can operate profitably in one neighborhood?" Other
Koreans purchased or opened a variety of small businesses including liquor stores
and dry cleaners. In Atlanta, Georgia, for example, the *Journal and Constitution*
observed, "Drop a load of dirty clothes at practically any dry cleaners and the business owner is likely to be Asian—Korean actually."

Korean establishments in the United States are concentrated in three large
metropolitan areas: Los Angeles, New York, and Chicago. Financially successful
Koreans left the inner cities when they could. They were concerned about their
children's futures, thought that the local public schools were neither safe nor aca-
demically sufficient, and often moved to the suburbs. Like the Chinese immigrants, Koreans established weekend classes for their children to promote their
cultural values as well as to prepare their students for admission to prestigious
Ivy League colleges or state universities such as the University of California at
Berkeley. By the end of the 1980s over 500 Korean language schools existed, 254
in the Los Angeles area alone. These ethnic establishments taught about college
entrance exams while keeping their children within the fold. Schools inculcated
knowledge and promoted a sense of self-confidence.

Half the Korean immigrants are Protestants, chiefly Methodists and
Presbyterians, despite coming from a land where Christians represented only 20
percent of the population. Many of the non-Christian Korean immigrants converted to Christianity after they arrived in America.

Korean churches were supportive institutions. As a leading scholar of Korean
immigrants explained, go to any city "where a sizeable number of Koreans live
and you are bound to find many Korean churches." Koreans even established congregations in neighborhoods where few of them lived. They located Protestant
houses of worship with declining memberships, took them over, and established
Korean language churches. These churches have become the focal point of the
Korean community and almost always provided special programs for the younger
generation.

FILIPINOS

Over three million Filipinos, 20 percent of whom have arrived in the past decade, live in the United States. Half reside in California, most are well educated, and they constitute the nation's largest group of Asian immigrants from one country. The United States acquired the Philippine Islands at the end of the Spanish American War in 1898; it gave the nation its independence in 1946. Throughout the twentieth century American movies, products, and fads penetrated the Filipino culture, and their public schools not only were patterned after American practices but used English as the language of instruction. As a result, Filipino immigrants knew about American folkways, mores, and popular lifestyles. Two-thirds of the new arrivals in the United States spoke English, and nearly half of Filipino men, and a majority of the women, had college or professional degrees.

Many of the newcomers were physicians who earned more money in the United States than they could have in the Philippines. An estimated nine thousand doctors had gone to the United States by 1980. Trained Filipino women could use their skills in many countries where economic opportunities abounded. For decades nurses had been leaving the islands and ministering to patients on different continents. Scholars have labeled these nurses "an Empire of Caring." Since the 1960s American hospitals, especially those in the inner cities, lacked sufficient numbers of nurses and actively recruited Filipinas. Because hospitals could not obtain enough nurses they continually pressured Congress to admit more of them. Congress also established Medicare and Medicaid, the same year it passed the Hart-Celler Act. These new medical programs increased the need for both physicians and nurses.

Overall, one-third of all Filipinas in the labor force were connected to health care. A doctor at New York City's Montefiore Hospital remarked, "If you meet a Filipino man he'll probably say 'My wife is a nurse.'" Another staff member at the same hospital stated, "If you meet a Filipino girl [sic] and say, 'you're a nurse' you're probably right." Because of their skills, and the need for those talents in the United States, women constituted 60 percent of all Filipino immigrants. Some foreign physicians even retrained as nurses; nursing visas for the United States were much easier to obtain than those for physicians.

In the 1970s the Philippine government established the Overseas Employment Development Board (OEDB) to encourage overseas employment of its citizens. It was done not only to minimize domestic unemployment but to foster economic growth as well. Migration meant that more money would flow into the nation's coffers, because the emigrants would send remittances to their relatives at home. These overseas workers were often called "OFWs," or overseas Filipino workers. The Philippine immigrants, whether in the United States or the Near East, were part of a global trend. Indeed, many emerging nations relied on the funds of emigrants to make life more bearable in countries where wages were low and poverty common.

The United States appealed because other Filipinos had prospered in the American economy. The newcomers headed for places where jobs were available. About half of them settled in California, where Filipino household incomes were considerably above the American national average. Living in mixed ethnic neighborhoods brought them into contact with other immigrants and American citizens, and since most Filipinos were Roman Catholic their participation in church activities also facilitated Americanization. Being well educated, earning above-average incomes, and worshiping with other Roman Catholics resulted in Filipinos having the highest rate of intermarriage of the post-1980s Asian immigrants.

Along with the "brain drain" of well-educated professionals from the Philippine Islands came working-class migrants, including those with visitor visas. They remained after their visas expired, thereby becoming illegal immigrants. The unauthorized extension of these "tourists" became such a problem that the American embassy in Manila responded by making visitor permits difficult to obtain. Some women were so eager to leave their homes that they sought American husbands through ads in American newspapers and on the Web. Filipinas were not the only nationality to use such "marriage bride" services, but they were the largest group engaging in this activity.

AN IMMIGRANT'S TALE

Florita Williams left school at an early age in the Philippines. She explained, "My family was so poor and they needed me to work." And work she did, mostly for low pay and long hours. She worked in the cane fields, as a maid, and as a babysitter, before moving to Manila at age sixteen. She met her husband there, but his death at an early age left her with a child to support and little money to do so. Her family cared for her child for five years while she worked long hours and under appalling conditions in a factory. Then a friend convinced her to publish a website designed to connect internationally.

Horace Williams Jr. found her website and became convinced that she was a lovely and sincere person. He wrote to her. Their relationship developed on the Internet. American immigration authorities frowned on this practice, believing that "mail order" marriages, especially in the Philippines, made a sham of the immigration laws. But eventually the government granted them the right to marry, which permitted her to come to America. She then came to the United States as Williams's wife and settled in Starksboro, Vermont, a place quite different from the Philippines. The couple encouraged her family back in the Philippines to pursue their education and then decided that it was Florita's turn to complete hers. It was hard for her to reenter school after thirty years. It was not easy for her. However, in 2008 Florita at long last received her diploma through a special Vermont adult learning program.

Many of the Filipino immigrants who had emigrated hoped to return home after the dictatorial regime of Ferdinand Marcos was overthrown in 1986. But economic conditions on the islands did not improve, life remained harsh, and many of the well-educated who had remained realized that they, too, had to leave to secure better lives. One teacher noted, "For those who have lost faith, the answer is going overseas. You don't join a political organization, you line up at an embassy."

VIETNAMESE REFUGEES

In the mid-1970s south Asians joined the eclectic mix of people seeking entry to the United States. More than half a million American troops had joined those of the South Vietnamese government fighting against the North Vietnamese and local communists in the 1960s. Despite the massive number of troops, no significant changes had occurred. By the late 1960s most Americans were fed up with the quagmire in Vietnam. Shortly after his inauguration, on January 20, 1969, President Richard Nixon began withdrawing American forces, and by 1973 they were practically gone. Two years later North Vietnamese communists launched effective attacks that quickly brought down the American-backed South Vietnamese government. Americans watched as thousands tried to escape in the helicopters that picked them up from the top of the American embassy and ferried them to American ships and possessions in the Pacific. Many others hired boats to take them from Vietnam to safety in other nations. Pirates attacked some of the ships, stole the refugees' money, and raped the women. In addition, neighboring countries were not eager to accept the Vietnamese. Thousands of others fled across the border into refugee camps in Thailand. The camps were unhealthy and even dangerous, but some Vietnamese lingered there for years until they were finally taken to the United States, Canada, Australia, and other nations.

Between 1975 and 1979 about 200,000 Vietnamese reached the United States, and in 1980 an additional 168,000 entered. By 2000 over a million Vietnamese had reached American shores. More than half settled in California, while large groups also established communities in Washington, DC, Houston, and Seattle. The first groups to leave Vietnam from 1975–1977 were well-educated people connected to the American military, the South Vietnamese government, or American businesses. A disproportionately large number were Roman Catholics who spoke English. Almost a quarter of the first batch of Vietnamese immigrants were classified as professional, technical, or managerial workers; 5 percent were farmers and fishermen. The Vietnamese had been accustomed to changing circumstances in their country, as they had at one time been part of French-controlled Indochina, and in the United States acculturated quickly while moving up the socioeconomic ladder at a faster pace than many previous Asian newcomers.

Another wave of Vietnamese emigrants left the country in 1978, when many ethnic Chinese also fled, some escaping by boat and others by crossing over the border into Thailand. A majority of these refugees had not completed high school, and practically all of them reported difficulty speaking English. The Thai government was not enthusiastic about welcoming them but established primitive camps for those who arrived. The United States and other nations finally agreed to accept a large number of the refugees stranded in the camps and eventually worked with the new communist state in Vietnam to organize the refugees into an "Orderly Departure Program." The program had mixed success in the 1980s. In addition, Congress passed the 1987 Amerasian Homecoming Act to bring orphans fathered by American soldiers who had been in Vietnam in the 1960s and 1970s to the United States. About sixty thousand teenagers and some of their relatives entered under this act. Raised as outcasts in Vietnam and often arriving without

AN IMMIGRANT'S TALE

One elderly woman who eventually went to America told her story to an interviewer:

I didn't want to leave Vietnam, but all of my children were gone; I'm old, and they have to take care of me. So I had to follow them.... The main problem I have in America is that I don't know how to speak English. Second, if I wanted to go somewhere, I cannot. I would have to use a car, but I cannot drive. If I use the bus, I am afraid that I will become lost. I have lots of barriers. If I have to fill out papers, I cannot. I also am unable to answer the phone. I know how to take down phone numbers, just a little, not much. If it were peaceful, I would live in Vietnam. I would live in the countryside because I have property and fields near the river, also a big garden with lots of fruit....

Children over here don't take care of their parents. In Vietnam, if poor, a person lived with his children; if rich, with only one child, possibly the youngest. Life was much more comfortable if [the rich] children and grandchildren would take care of you.... The difference is that over here children do not obey their parents; in Vietnam, they obeyed us more. Over here, whenever we say something, they like to argue. My husband and I dislike this. If our children want something and we don't like it, they will not listen to us. Things we consider to be right they consider wrong.

No matter what might happen, no matter where we would have landed or stayed, we had to leave Vietnam, not only for America, but for anywhere. If my husband had remained in Vietnam, the Communists would have arrested and killed him. Therefore we had to go. We left everything behind.[1]

---

1. Source: James M. Freeman, *Hearts of Sorrow: The Vietnamese Lives* (Stanford: Stanford University Press, 1989), 371–375.

families in America, they found the adjustment difficult. But life could also be hard on older refugees as well.

Social service organizations and the US government collaborated to settle the refugees throughout the nation. The newcomers were not required to remain where they had been placed, and many resettled in California. Orange County, just south of Los Angeles, became the center of Vietnamese life and culture in the United States. As early as 1990 "Little Saigon" became the common name for the city of Westminster. Some eight hundred shops catered to the new Vietnamese immigrants. One Vietnamese American developer reflected, "The Chinese, the Japanese, the Italians and the Jews grouped together when they came to the US. There seemed to be no reason why the Vietnamese wouldn't follow suit."

CAMBODIAN REFUGEES

While the Vietnamese were by far the largest refugee group from south Asia, the war in Vietnam of the 1960s–1970s engulfed both Cambodia and Laos as well. The triumph of a radical regime in Cambodia led to a virtual holocaust under the government of the Khmer Rouge and its leader, Pol Pot. The regime of Pol Pot slaughtered over one million Cambodians who were believed to be opposed to the regime or who stood in the way of radical reforms to remake Cambodia. Beginning in the late 1970s, thousands fled the terror of the Khmer Rouge and crossed into Thailand to escape the horror of their daily lives. Pol Pot's regime was ultimately overthrown by an invading Vietnamese army. Several hundred thousand Cambodians eventually settled in the United States.

Unlike the Vietnamese, whose male and female emigrants were almost equal in numbers, among the Cambodians roughly one-quarter of families were headed by women because so many of the men had been killed by the Khmer Rouge. The wretched lives of Cambodians before emigrating made it difficult for them to adjust in the United States. They often had to take menial jobs or resort to welfare to keep their heads afloat. Preserving their cultural customs helped their survival, but for women who headed households and did not speak English well, the new environment was harsh. The importance of Buddhism to the lives of Cambodians was demonstrated by the fact that one of the first things they did after they settled was to build a Buddhist temple.

LAOTIAN REFUGEES

A third refugee group created by the Vietnam War came from Laos. About two hundred thousand came to the United States; about half of them were the Hmong, who had aided the United States during the war. They too feared for their futures when the communists took over. The first to flee were soldiers who had fought on the American side. Most came in the 1980s and the 1990s, but the migration slowed after that. The Hmong settled mostly in Minneapolis, but they also established communities in Wisconsin, California, and other areas.

Like Cambodians, they had difficulty adjusting to their new lives in the United States. Few were English speakers, and most lacked the job skills needed in the United States. Even though many had aided the American forces during the Vietnamese War, Congress at first was reluctant to assist these former allies. Nonetheless, legislators finally provided refugee benefits to them. The Hmong became the largest group of Asians on welfare and, along with the Cambodians, they were the two Asian groups most likely to be emotionally depressed and report marital strife. Because of these factors, their distinct cultures, and their uprooting, the Hmong community remained somewhat segregated.

RECEPTION OF ASIAN IMMIGRANTS

The growth of Asian communities has been generally accepted by other Americans. The elite newcomers usually found employment and income commensurate with their skills, and they have been able to move to upscale suburban communities, with their children attending schools for the gifted and talented in places like New York City and elsewhere. However, some Asians have complained that there is a glass ceiling for promotion in American businesses, and many believe that they have encountered job discrimination. They have also insisted that elite colleges and universities such as Harvard have quotas against Asians, but the US Civil Rights Commission was unable find evidence of such discrimination.

Affirmative Action to assist minorities and others needing a helping hand began in the late 1960s and early 1970s. Originally intended as a stepping stone for African Americans, it resulted in assistance to groups not considered when the practice became part of public policies. Unfortunately, Affirmative Action resulted in unexpected debates, conflicts, and charges that Asian and Caucasian individuals were being discriminated against through no fault of their own. After 1990 the protests intensified. When the University of California eliminated Affirmative Action in college and graduate school admissions, and based freshmen acceptances solely on SAT scores and high school grades, the number of Asians admitted to the state's elite universities increased, while admissions for Hispanics and African Americans decreased.

But Asians were victimized by other kinds of bigotry: violent attacks. The US Civil Rights Commission has documented a number of discriminatory incidents, and local communities have reported hate crimes directed at them. In New Jersey, for example, a group of young men sought out and attacked Asian Indians and in 1987 murdered one Asian Indian. The youth called themselves "Dot Busters," a reference to the fact that some Indian women wear a red dot on their forehead as a sign of marital fidelity. Vincent Chin died in Detroit in 1992 after being brutalized by some unemployed autoworkers. They believed that he was Japanese and therefore made him the victim of their wrath because they thought the growing number of Japanese cars in the United States were responsible for losing their jobs at auto plants. Although the autoworkers beat Chin to death with baseball bats they were only fined and given suspended sentences. The Chin case catalyzed Asian

Americans who urged strong governmental action to prosecute persons guilty of such crimes, and after the 1990s such incidents declined as Asian Americans found more acceptance in American society. Declined but not entirely gone. In August 2012 a gunman entered a Sikh temple near Milwaukee and killed six people who had come to worship. Moreover, some Asian Americans noted that even after the incident Asians were often seen as outsiders.

MIDDLE EASTERNERS

Still another group of people impacted by the Immigration Act of 1965 were residents in the Middle East, although their numbers were only one tenth as many as South and East Asians. Although immigrants from Middle Eastern nations had been increasing after 1965, they did not become visible to other Americans until the 1990s. After 1965, newly independent nations such as Egypt, Israel, Jordan, and Syria received the same limited quota of twenty thousand immigrants annually, but they rarely utilized their full allotments.

The Middle East had vast deposits of oil, but not all Middle Easterners shared the profits. Since the establishment of Israel in 1948, wars with her Arab neighbors seemed almost endless, and left thousands of non-Jews homeless or with limited means to support themselves. Rapid population growth in Egypt, which lacked oil, taxed existing resources. In Turkey economic growth also lagged as the population grew; indeed, many Turks went to Germany as guest workers to send badly needed funds home. Lebanon was deeply divided, and whole neighborhoods in Beirut, its capital, were destroyed during a civil war in the 1970s. Plagued by constant wars and violence, hundreds of thousands of Middle Easterners left their homelands in search of jobs and safety. Oil-rich Near Eastern states needed labor, hence they recruited both skilled and unskilled workers within and outside of the region. Some were medical professionals, such as Filipina nurses. Others were recruited to fill unskilled jobs. These migrants were temporary workers. In August 1990, Iraq invaded Kuwait and soon expelled many of these immigrants. This invasion led to the first Gulf War in 1991.

Troubled Middle Easterners represented a wide diversity of people. Arabs constituted the largest group of Middle Eastern immigrants to enter the United States after the 1970s. Most of them came from Egypt, Lebanon, Iraq, or Jordan, but there were also a number of Palestinians, who may have exceeded one hundred thousand. Many Palestinians entered with Jordanian passports, but told census takers in 1990 that they were Palestinians. Perhaps as many 15 percent of those entering as Israelis were Israeli Arabs.

Not all immigrants from the Middle East hailed from an Arabic or Islamic culture. Although most Arabs were Muslims, substantial minorities included Christians, Jews, and smaller religious groups. Christians were also divided. Egyptian Copts were among the oldest Christians. Christians from Lebanon often converted to Roman Catholicism once in the United States, but Armenian Christians had their own churches in both the United States and the Middle East.

Many Middle Eastern migrants to America possessed marketable skills. Some had already been to the United States as students. They included highly educated professionals like lawyers, professors and other teachers, engineers, and physicians. These people had little difficulty finding employment, and many married American citizens. Turkey, too, sent many of its elite to study and/or to live in America. The largest settlement of Arab immigrants formed in New York City, but the center of Arabic culture was Detroit, and especially nearby Dearborn. In Dearborn one could find Arabic newspapers, shops, and groceries, and hear Arabic spoken on the streets.

Israeli immigrants, in general, were well educated. They were often called *yordim*, which was a pejorative name other Israelis pinned on emigrants. Israel needed more Jewish immigrants and frowned on citizens who abandoned the country. Many Jews also fled from North Africa and Iraq during the years of conflict between Israel and her neighbors. The exact number of Israelis in the United States is difficult to determine. Like so many other immigrants who came as tourists or temporary workers, some remained in the United States illegally. Estimates have placed as many as one hundred thousand Israelis living in the United States at the end of the 1990s.

Iran also stood out for its immigration patterns and potential future immigration. The Iranian migration also illustrated the continuing connection between foreign policy and immigration. In 1953 a coup orchestrated by the US Central Intelligence Agency (CIA) and Great Britain overthrew a nationalist leader in Iran and replaced him with Mohammed Reza Shah, who was strongly anticommunist and willing to protect British and American oil interests. Upper- and middle-class Iranians also profited from the shah's policies. Many prosperous Iranians sent their children to colleges and universities in the United States to acquire technical skills needed in their homeland's economy. Some of these students either married Americans or found employment that enabled them to remain in the United States. However, the vast majority of students returned to Iran, and immigration from Iran barely exceeded an average of one thousand persons a year from 1950 to 1980. Most Iranians, however, did not share in their country's growth, and Muslim religious leaders surged to the fore. Led by clerics, Iran experienced an Islamic revolution in 1979. In that year, the revolutionaries seized over fifty members of the American embassy staff and created a diplomatic crisis that was not resolved until January 20, 1981, the day of Ronald Reagan's inauguration as president.

After the fall of the shah in 1978, and the successful religious revolution, an exodus of Iranians headed either for Western Europe or the United States. At the time that the Revolutionary Islamic Republic was established, thirty-six thousand Iranians were students in the United States. Rather than returning home, many decided to stay, and once becoming immigrants or citizens, they brought their relatives to join them. Starting with the ascension of Islamic clerics in 1979, the United States considered Iran a hostile power whose citizens were entitled to asylum. Because of the continued turmoil, some three hundred thousand immigrants from Iran were admitted to the United States between the late 1970s and

2010. Of these people, nearly one hundred thousand were brought in as refugees or given asylum (asylum was granted to people on an individual basis who were already in the United States. Refugees were brought into the United States from abroad). Although refugees from many parts of the world sought asylum, Iranians had one of the highest approval rates—about 50 percent—compared to only 2 or 3 percent for Central Americans.

The majority of Iranians entered the United States as regular immigrants. They were usually wealthy, well educated, and English speaking. Most of these Iranians were Muslims who did not share the values and practices of the new Islamic Iran. Also included in the larger flow from Iran were Jews, Armenians, and members of the Baha'i faith, who feared for their future in a radical Islamic Republic. The *Iran Times* asserted that one-third of the nation's physicians and dentists left after the Islamic revolution. One survey found that Iranian men had higher levels of education than Iranian women. However, over 40 percent of Iranian women in Los Angeles had obtained college degrees.

Like all immigrants, these latest migrants tried to maintain their cultures while integrating into American life. Few believed they would ever return to Iran. In Iran women usually did not work for wages, but in the United States their labor participation rates were close to those of American norms. Iranians also published ethnic newspapers and operated a television station in Farsi, a dialect common in Iran, which beamed news to those in the Middle East with television sets that could receive it.

Still another Middle Eastern group in the United States emigrated from Afghanistan. In 1979 Soviet troops entered that country to support an unpopular communist government. In retaliation for what he saw as untoward aggression President Jimmy Carter canceled American participation in the Olympics, which were to be held in Moscow in 1980, and gave aid to help the Afghanis resist the invaders. By doing so, Americans aligned themselves with a variety of native organizations including the Taliban, a radical Islamic group. After a decade of war, the Soviet troops left, but fighting continued among various Afghani tribes. As the bloody conflict continued, several thousand Afghans sought refuge in the United States. The American government granted many of them asylum and refugee status.

The main religion of Afghanistan is Islam, and these Afghan immigrants were mostly Muslims, but otherwise were not representative of the nation's population. They were usually middle-class and well-educated immigrants who had the means, connections, and knowledge to flee. Or, as one observer noted, "The cream of the crop of Afghan society migrated to the U.S. or Europe." In spite of their talents and abilities Afghan immigrants often had to begin their working lives abroad at the bottom of the economy.

Like many other immigrant groups, Afghans established tight-knit communities. The largest is in the San Francisco Bay area. Across the bay from San Francisco, a Fremont neighborhood became known as "Little Kabul" because of the presence of so many Afghan restaurants and shops.

In 1989 the Cold War ended in Europe. Violent conflicts continued in the Middle East, and economic pressure for Latinos to migrate resulted in record numbers of new immigrants going to the United States. America had a generous immigration policy, which became more generous after the passage of the Immigration Act of 1990. From middle of the 1990s to the end of the century, the America economy expanded. Thus all the stars aligned by 1990 to encourage the entry of over twenty million people to the United States in the next two decades. This was the largest number of immigrants ever recorded in a twenty year period since the nation began in 1789.

CHAPTER 4

The Era of Latinos, 1965–2012

Latinos, or Hispanics, constitute about one-half, and a majority of the undocumented, immigrants to the United States in recent decades. In 2005, Mexico's share of the immigrant population outnumbered the combined totals of newcomers from the next four nations: the Philippines, India, China, and Vietnam (Figure 4.1). A number of factors stimulated this flow: wars, revolutions, tyrannical governments in their home countries, and family unification. The most important determinant, however, was economic opportunity. An overwhelming majority of people have moved from one nation to another because they believed that by doing so they would improve the quality of their lives. While Western Europe has benefited from the exodus of individuals from less developed countries to more industrialized ones, no other nation has received as many immigrants as the United States.

Mexicans, although heavily concentrated in the West and Southwest, live in every region of the nation. There are large communities in cities such as Houston, Los Angeles, San Diego, Chicago, and Dallas. And from 1990 to 2011 over three hundred thousand Mexicans headed to New York City, where they joined other Latinos such as Dominicans and Puerto Ricans, who are native-born citizens. Mexicans have also been drawn to smaller cities and towns where chicken or meat processing plants were located. Moreover, they joined many newcomers in the nation's suburbs. In other words, Mexicans, Latinos, and other immigrants went where the jobs were located.

In the South, Latinos accounted for only 3.8 percent of the southern population in 1990, and that percentage has since doubled. This dramatic growth in southern diversity led some quipsters to label the "New South" as the "Nuevo South." In the past decade South Carolina, Alabama, and Tennessee have ranked among the fastest-growing Hispanic states. Between 2000 and 2006, South Carolina's Latino population rose 51 percent. At the beginning of the twenty-first century Arkansas witnessed a 48 percent increase in its Mexican population, which led the Mexican

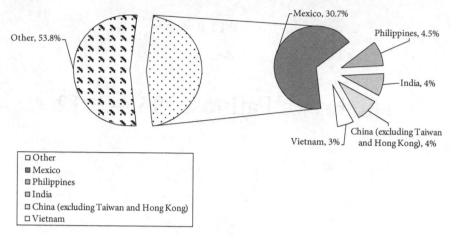

- Other
- Mexico
- Philippines
- India
- China (excluding Taiwan and Hong Kong)
- Vietnam

Figure 4.1 Top Five Countries of Origin of the Foreign-Born Population Living in the United States (2005)

SOURCE: Bureau of the Census, 2006.

government to open a consulate in Little Rock. After the new consul arrived, he noted the expanding Mexican-owned businesses and remarked: "This is like the birth of a community."

Mexican immigrants can also be found in the Rocky Mountain states, the Midwest, and the Northeast. Nevada witnessed more than a 50 percent increase in its Hispanic population since 2000. Many political observers credited the group with providing the decisive margin of victory for Senator Harry Reid's reelection in 2010. In Vermont the dairy industry employed Mexican migrants to milk cows twice a day. In 2008, a federal crackdown on illegal immigrants in Vermont drew the ire of the dairy farmers, and as a result, one of Vermont's US Senators introduced a bill in Congress to legalize the status of the workers.

Sometime in the late twentieth century Spanish surpassed Italian and German as the foreign language most often spoken at home. The census reported that "Garcia" and "Rodriguez" were catching up with "Smith" as the most common surnames in the largest cities of the United States. The leading TV station in Miami was Spanish-language, and other cities operated Spanish-speaking networks as well. Several groups opposed to large-scale immigration backed propositions to make English the official language of their states. However, businesses thought differently: many telephone books were published in both languages, and anyone making phone calls for airline tickets and other services found that voices on automated systems asked callers whether they wished to continue in Spanish or English. Moreover, in 2007, Atlanta, Georgia, celebrated the Mexican national holiday, *Cinco de Mayo*, at the Plaza Fiesta Mall. "It's like you've been transported to Mexico," said the mall's general manager. Another official remarked, "To survive in retailing, you have to market to Hispanics and Asians."

Photo 4-1 Many Ethnic Groceries Have Appeared in Recent Years. This One is Offering Mexican Food

BACKGROUND

In the 1965 Immigration Act Congress limited annual immigration from the Western Hemisphere to 120,000. However, in 1976 Congress and the attorney general exempted Cubans from the ceiling. In the late 1970s modifications to the law created a worldwide system of immigration that limited each nation to no more than twenty thousand persons annually, not counting immediate family members of US citizens. Exempting immediate family members from quotas helped all immigrants. Mexico could not have sent 150,000 annually in the 2000s without this provision in the 1965 immigration act. Of Mexico's 138,717 immigrants in 2010, 86,328 were immediate family members of American citizens. Laws such as the Immigration Reform and Control Act of 1986 (IRCA), which granted an amnesty for 2.7 million illegal aliens, also helped increase Latino immigration; Mexicans alone accounted for over half of those who benefited from the amnesty. In addition, the Nicaraguan and Central American Relief Act of 1997 (NCARA) also gave an amnesty to tens of thousands of Central Americans who arrived before 1997. Even these changes, however, proved inadequate to meet the numbers of people who wanted to migrate north; as a result, millions arrived without documents after these acts expired (Figure 4.2).

US foreign policy and violence also played a role in Hispanic immigration. The United States had been interested in the affairs of Latin America since the

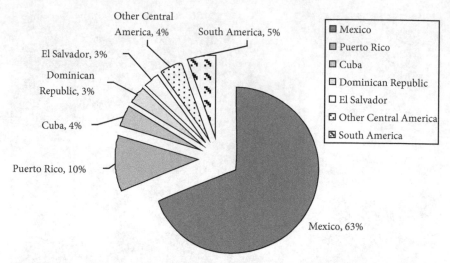

Figure 4.2 Latino Population of the United States by Place of Origin, 2006
SOURCE: Department of Homeland Security (DHS), *Statistical Yearbook*, 2006.

1820s, when President James Monroe issued a doctrine declaring that America had a special interest in the Western Hemisphere and did not want European interference. The United States intervened numerous times in the Caribbean between 1900 and 1933. President Franklin D. Roosevelt's so-called Good Neighbor policy, started in 1934, suggested that the United States might keep out of Latin American affairs, but the Cold War that developed between the United States and the Soviet Union after 1945 led to new interventions.

One cannot overlook the factors that propelled thousands to move north after 1945. Poverty at home and much higher wages in the United States certainly affected the exodus. Civil wars in Central America also left many homeless and with little chance for adequate employment. Civil unrest, violence related to the drug trade, and economic troubles meant that most Mexicans coming to the United States, whether legal or not, had strong incentives to leave home and seek a better future.

The Mexican economy after 1980 experienced a sharp devaluation of the peso and a bust in the oil industry. In 1994 the North American Free Trade Agreement (NAFTA) intensified economic difficulties for Mexican farmers. Under NAFTA, Mexican farm products competed with more efficient and lower priced agricultural commodities from the United States. Thus, in spite of a declining birthrate in Mexico after 1990 there was good reason to head north, where wages were at least five times greater.

The southwestern states and Mexico share a border of nearly two thousand miles, yet for many Mexicans the line of demarcation has little meaning. For decades after the United States acquired the northern half of Mexico as the prize of the Mexican-American War in 1848, Mexicans and Americans frequently crossed the boundaries of each nation without even knowing it. After annexation, those who lived in the annexed area were given the option of becoming American citizens. The United States did not have a border patrol until 1924, and the existence of an insufficient number of officers was hardly a barrier to immigration. During the prohibition era of the 1920s, the Border Patrol's main concern was to halt the liquor trade.

As noted, during World War II a program was created to bring temporary workers from Mexico to do the work that the young men drafted into war service would have done. The Braceros came legally under a mutual agreement between Mexico and the United States, but many others arrived without documents to perform menial jobs as farm laborers or as maintenance workers on the railroads. Thus it was quite natural for Mexicans to cross into the United States in search of higher wages, since their grandparents and parents had done that before them.

As in the case of Europeans, there were options for Latinos other than moving to the United States. If the economies and wars in their own countries triggered desires to find a better life, then emigrants turned to South American nations for security and a chance of higher wages. Venezuela, for example, had a relatively liberal immigration policy, especially for Colombians escaping the violence of the drug wars of their country. Some South Americans of Spanish heritage migrated to Spain, while the descendants of Japanese immigrants in South America went to Japan. Brazilians left for Portugal, and many from Argentina headed for Italy. Caribbean people emigrated to Canada and Great Britain. Authorities believe that in the 2000s migration increased among Latin American countries. Some of the migrations were only temporary, with workers crossing boundaries for short-term employment, usually to harvest crops. However, low wages and unsettled political conditions in many Latin American nations stimulated movement, and wages in the United States were always higher.

MEXICANS

Mexicans account for almost two-thirds of the Hispanic population in the United States (Figure 4.3) and over 60 percent of the undocumented immigrants. After the terrorist attacks on September 11, 2001, it became harder to get into the United States. Tighter controls along California's border with Mexico forced many hopeful migrants to try entering through Arizona. Undocumented immigrants crossing the desert to Arizona risked dying of sunstroke and dehydration in the summer months, when daily temperatures exceed one hundred degrees. In years gone by, some undocumented migrants trying to reach the United States through Texas or New Mexico had drowned in the Rio Grande River; now they perished in the desert. Although there are no statistics available, it is estimated that over one thousand would-be immigrants perished in the desert from 1993 to 2002, and more than one thousand since that date (Figure 4.4).

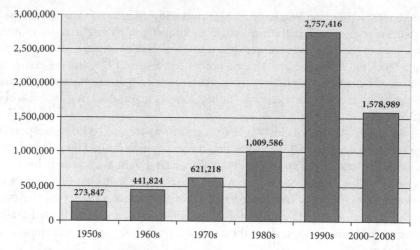

Figure 4.3 Legal Immigration from Mexico by Decades
SOURCE: DHS, *Statistical Yearbook,* 2009.

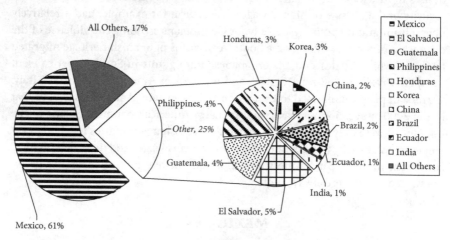

Figure 4.4 Source of Undocumented Immigration, 2008
SOURCE: DHS, *Statistical Yearbook,* 2008.

In *Dying to Cross: The Worst Immigrant Tragedy in American History* (2005), author George Ramos relates the tale of seventy-three people trying to reach the United States in 2003. After crossing the border, they were loaded into a tightly sealed tractor-trailer with no air conditioning, and headed three hundred miles north to Houston, Texas, to find jobs. Mostly Latinos, the largest number in the group was from Mexico. The driver made one stop to get the passengers water, but on a particularly hot day he then abandoned them in the truck. When the van was discovered and opened, nineteen persons had already died, and many others were suffering from heat exhaustion. The youngest victim was only five years old. Survivors had punched several holes in the truck, and the passengers took turns getting to the holes so they could breathe. Eventually authorities found the driver and several of the "coyotes" (people who smuggled migrants into the United States for a fee) involved in the scheme and brought them to justice. Despite the life-threatening possibilities, desperate people without appropriate documents still try to cross the border into the United States. In July 2012, even after the numbers attempting to enter without documents dropped sharply, fourteen undocumented immigrants were killed when a truck carrying them crashed in Texas.

There are other ways for Mexicans to get to America. The United States issues Border Crossing Cards (BCC) to qualified Mexicans, which enables them to shop or visit legally in the United States for up to seventy-two hours. Like the Poles and Irish who entered on tourist visas in the eastern United States, or Greek sailors who abandoned their ships once they docked in American harbors, many BCC holders remain in the United States indefinitely. The federal government labels those who abuse their entry privileges "overstayers" or "visa abusers."

One creative way for foreigners to gain entry is through participation in sporting events. Mexican soccer clubs often receive invitations to compete with American teams in Houston and other cities. Players then obtain temporary visas to enter the United States. Previous Mexican immigrants entertained these foreign visiting athletes while telling them of the opportunities in the city. When the buses returned to Mexico, they left with fewer persons than when they came, as several players decided to stay and try their luck in America.

A great incentive for immigrants to remain and work in the United States is to lessen the poverty that Mexican families face at home. Once they find jobs in the United States, they live frugally, especially if they are undocumented, and send money to their families back home. Often they live together in cramped quarters to keep their expenses down. Ricardo Morales, a twenty-six-year-old roofer, told a reporter in 2008 that he had lived in Chicago for four years. He earned $500 weekly and sent $400 home monthly. He claimed that his remittances were responsible for turning his parents' Mexican "shack of tin" into a "three bedroom concrete house." In addition, he had a bank account in the United States that would be used to send his brother to college. "Our thinking," he said, "is that we will make sacrifices now so that our families can live better and so that one day we will live better back home."

How much money is sent to Mexico from the United States is not known precisely, but it runs into the billions of dollars annually. Remittances constitute Mexico's third-largest source of income, after oil exports and tourism. The World Bank estimates that global remittances were at least $235 billion in 2007, with $28 billion going to Mexico. In 2010, the World Bank increased its estimate for that year to $325 billion, with about one-tenth of that amount heading to Mexico. Checks from Mexican migrants to their relatives averaged $350 per transaction between 2005 and 2008. Just how important remittances were is revealed in a 2005 analysis of villages in Oaxaca, Mexico. Half of the residents reported that they received money from America. While the Mexican government and some econo-mists wanted to use the money for investment, the recipients reported that 60 per-cent was used for household expenses. A remittance of $700 every two months was necessary to pay for basic appliances or home improvements. However, the reces-sion in the United States that began in 2007 in construction affected how much money was sent to Latin America in 2008. Whereas 73 percent of immigrants in Arizona sent money to relatives in 2006, only about half did so in 2008.

One difficulty of remitting money is the fee charged by Western Union. Many Mexicans do not have official government identification; over half of the unau-thorized migrants lack bank accounts. In 2003 the Mexican consulates in the United States began issuing ID cards, called matricula consular cards, to Mexican citizens abroad. These were not accepted by the United States or state agencies as official documents; however, American banks accepted them when the presenter opened a bank account, thus making it easier to send money home and purchase goods in America.

Moreover, immigrants developed alternative schemes to get money home. If one were a legal immigrant or US citizen, one could legally travel from the United States to Mexico and personally deliver cash. Couriers charged for the service, but the fee was usually lower than using established methods such as Western Union. To be sure, the United States has limits about how much money could be taken out, but cars or trucks heading for Mexico are rarely searched.

To send money home immigrants needed jobs that enabled them to save. Becoming a skilled worker, as in the case of roofer Ricardo Morales, was an achievement. Mexican immigrants, with or without documents, usually face sev-eral barriers when entering the American job market. On the whole they are less well educated than their American counterparts; less than one-half of them have finished high school, compared to nearly 90 percent of Americans who have. Put another way, the average Mexican has completed 8.5 years of schooling, while the American average is 12.2 years. Compared to immigrants from Asia, Europe, and Africa, Mexicans are much less likely to be college graduates. Overall, studies indi-cate that the undocumented immigrants are not as educationally accomplished as those entering with legal documents. Often many lack English. As a result, they take lower-paying jobs. Many men work as janitors in large office buildings. In California, these jobs pay better wages than in most other states. Some jobs pro-vided them with union benefits such as regulated working hours and health care.

For women, poor education and language skills often led to work as maids in motels, hotels, and private homes. While the garment industry in general is declin-ing in the United States, cities such as Los Angeles still have many shops that need minimally skilled or unskilled workers. Such places resemble the sweatshops of the past with their long hours, unsanitary conditions, and low pay.

Another way for men to earn needed dollars is to stand on street corners wait-ing for someone to hire day workers. The first national survey of day laborers car-ried out in the mid-2000s revealed that pay for them was typically around ten to twenty dollars per hour, although many were paid even less. They could not count

Photo 4-2 New Jersey Library Offers Citizenship Classes

on finding work five days a week. In Agoura Hills, California, the laborers banded together and insisted that they be paid fifteen dollars per hour. Elsewhere, other groups set minimums of eight to ten dollars per hour. Even the better paying jobs carry risks: basic worker protections are often unenforced, many employers do not grant food and water breaks, and some unscrupulous employers refuse to pay workers as promised. Because they usually "lacked papers," undocumented workers fear to take complaints to local governmental officials. Day laborers also encounter community hostility in some areas. Many towns provide them with space and facilities for hiring, but in other communities, day workers are accused of being an unsightly appearance on street corners. In Farmingdale, New York, two day laborers were assaulted in 2000 after being lured into a building with the promise of work.

While work in construction pays well, it also carries several risks. First, there is the chance of injury. Second, workers are subject to the vicissitudes of the economy. From the first quarter of 2006 to the first quarter of 2007, Hispanics found nearly 300,000 new jobs in construction, but then a housing slump resulted in the loss of 221,000 jobs. The decline in housing construction, combined with a tight economy, resulted in much higher rates of unemployment. Women were also affected by the downturn in the economy; high-paying jobs were lost by Anglos, who then reduced or eliminated household help.

Another critical source of jobs for Latino immigrants is the emerging meat and chicken processing industry throughout the United States, especially in the

"Nuevo South" and the Midwest. Many Mexicans took these jobs, even though the working conditions were poor and wages were only $7 or $8 an hour. Worker turnover was high, but employers always seemed to find replacements because so many faced even poorer conditions in Mexico.

An example of the terrible work environment came to light in 2008, when the Immigration and Customs Enforcement Agency (ICE) raided Agriprocessers, Inc., in Pottsville, Iowa. The appalling sweatshop conditions in the plant rivaled those that had existed at the end of the nineteenth and early twentieth centuries before state labor laws and unions forced employers to improve working conditions. In this case, most of the workers were from Guatemala. The government arrested and sent 270 employees to jail; they were charged with using fraudulent social security cards. After several months in jail, the undocumented workers were deported. In the follow-up of the raid, however, conditions in the workplace came to public light. Subsequently, both the federal and state governments investigated the plant for violations of existing labor laws. These inspections led to the discovery of over nine thousand violations including the employment of thirty-two children; the youngsters claimed that they worked up to seventeen hours a day on fast production lines using sharp knives to cut meat and chickens, a job for which they had received no training. A sixteen-year-old girl explained, "When you start, you can't stay awake. But after a while you get used to it." The federal government then prosecuted and convicted several of the employers for labor violations.

One of the worst stories of exploitation came to light in 1997, when sixty deaf Mexicans, including ten children, were discovered living in horrendous conditions in New York City. They had been smuggled from schools for the hearing impaired in Mexico with promises that they had a better life awaiting them in the United States. Instead they were forced to sell trinkets on the streets, in subways, and at airports. When authorities discovered the presence of these unfortunate people, the smugglers and people who ran this criminal enterprise were arrested and prosecuted.

One way to improve conditions was for the workers to form a union, but unionization along the "chicken trail"—as the poultry and meat processing industry was called—was difficult and rare. Moreover, the Hispanic influx began when unions were suffering major losses in the United States. In the 1950s, union members had represented over one-third of the work force, but by the 2000s, membership numbered only 11 percent of workers, and most American attitudes toward unions were commonly hostile or at best indifferent. Los Angeles hotels began to break their unions, which were dominated by African Americans, by using firms that paid workers poorly and were shunned by unionized crews. By the 1980s, hotel and aligned businesses had virtually destroyed the Service Employees International Union.

In 1986 the Justice for Janitors movement, composed mainly of Latinos, emerged to replace the old unions. This resurgence of organized labor produced contracts for many hotel- and office-cleaning workers in major cities such as Denver, Los Angeles, New York, and San Francisco. The major national unions then dropped their opposition to unionizing undocumented immigrants and began to organize them, though with only modest success. Immigrants, even those with documents, discovered how difficult it was to organize a union at the Palmero Pizza plant in Wisconsin. When they attempted to unionize in 2012 the company fired them.

An increase in raids and deportations of undocumented workers in industries known to employ many unauthorized immigrants contributed to the slowing of undocumented immigrants after 2007. Such raids, combined with the declining American economy, caused potential immigrants to think twice about heading to the United States. One immigrant explained, "Many friends of mine are thinking of going back in December [of 2008]. They are asking themselves, why stay here, there are no jobs and we don't have legal papers."

For the minority of legal Mexicans who had graduated from high school, gone to college, and acquired English language skills, white-collar employment opportunities existed. Their American-born children fared better; in 2006, the government reported that the median annual income for foreign-born Hispanics was $23,545, but the figure for members of the second generation was $30,689.

AN IMMIGRANT'S TALE

Alfredo Quinones-Hinojosa was born in Mexico in 1968. His father ran a small gas station. When the Mexican peso was devalued in the 1980s the family's income fell. He knew that his future was limited if he stayed home; hence he decided to do what many young Mexican men did: he left for the United States. Crossing as an illegal immigrant by "hopping over a fence," he found work on a farm, where he labored "seven days a week, sunup to sundown." Quinones-Hinojosa quickly realized that migrating to the United States did not solve his problems. He moved to Stockton, California, where he found employment that enabled him to attend classes at night at the local junior college. There he met a professor who encouraged him to pursue further education.

Quinones-Hinojosa applied to the University of California at Berkeley. As a student with a strong science background, he was informed that Hispanics with such high grades should not stop at the BA level, and he went on to attend Harvard Medical School. While at Harvard, where he became a US citizen, he discovered that he was interested in the functioning of the human brain and decided to become a brain surgeon. He moved to Johns Hopkins University Medical School, where he became one of the nation's top neurosurgeons, performing over two hundred operations a year. When asked by an interviewer if he had found Harvard difficult, he replied, "Not really. Compared to working in the fields it was easy."

Not only were Hispanic immigrants able to earn more money in the United States, but they also opened businesses catering to the Mexican community. In Walnut Park, California, near Los Angeles, a Hispanic-oriented shopping mall opened in 2008; in Texas, a partnership between local governmental agencies and businesses converted the Fort Worth Town Center into a Latino-themed mall. The head of Primestor Development, himself Hispanic, planned for several new malls around the country in the near future. He acknowledged receiving a growing number of phone calls about economic development in Mexican American communities: "People understand now that it is a very significant market they need to get educated on."

Of all institutions important to the growing Mexican immigrant community, none was as significant as the Roman Catholic Church. Mexico is a Catholic nation. Before the 1960s, Mexican newcomers generally settled in the American Southwest, where the Church was not as well established as it was in the eastern part of the United States. In the East and Midwest, Slavs, Irish, Germans, and Italians formed the majority of the Catholic Church's members. The Catholic Church in those regions also ran large parochial school systems to instruct children in moral values and religious doctrine. However, the Church had few schools in the Southwest. In addition, the Catholic Church was hit with a financial crisis, a pedophilia scandal, and a drastic shortage in the number of priests and nuns, especially Spanish-speaking ones, at the same time that Mexicans began to arrive in the United States in large numbers. As a result, many Mexicans did not feel that American Catholicism welcomed them. Not until April 2010 did the Church appoint a Mexican-born archbishop, Jose H. Gomez, to the Archdiocese of Los Angeles.

Within the Catholic Church, a major conflict developed over Mexican immigrants' belief in the Virgin of Guadalupe. According to Mexican tradition, the Virgin Mary appeared in a vision to a farmer in 1531 and told him that she wanted a Catholic Church built on Tepeyac Hill, the site of a former Aztec temple. This revelation touched off a wave of piety toward the Virgin of Guadalupe, a devotion that Mexicans carried with them to the United States. At first, the US Catholic Church hierarchy was not enthusiastic about this belief because it detracted from what it saw as traditional church teaching. Gradually, however, church leaders recognized how important the Virgin was to Mexican immigrants. In December 2008 a replica of the Virgin at the Mexico City Basilica was brought to New York City to be shown at St. Patrick's Cathedral. The city's Mexicans were thrilled. The *New York Times* reported that construction worker Jose Reyes got up at 4:30 a.m. to participate in a procession known as the Feast of Our Lady of Guadalupe. "It's indescribable what you feel when you're walking with her, knowing that she came all the way from where your roots began," he declared. More than one observer insisted that one was not truly Mexican if one did not believe in the Virgin of Guadalupe. Octavio Paz, a Nobel Prize–winning Mexican poet remarked, "After two centuries of experiment and failure, the Mexican people only believe in the Virgin of Guadalupe and the National Lottery." Women particularly valued "Our

Lady of Guadalupe," as she not only gave them the "strength to endure dehumanizing circumstances," but inspired them "by her dignity and push for greater public roles [for women]."

Pentecostal Christianity, which for several years had been expanding in part because of its appeal to the emotional needs of the poor and working classes began to draw Mexicans in the United States as well. One minister expressed its attraction for newcomers: "Our mission is to welcome the immigrant and be his guide and support. If they need money to pay the rent, we'll raise the money for them. If they need work, we'll find them work. If they need someone to talk to, they can come to me." There are no official figures, but in the late 2000s the Pew Foundation estimated that 1.3 million Latinos owed their allegiance to Pentecostal revivalism. This loss of congregants troubled the Catholic Church, which also worried that surveys from 2007 through 2010 indicated that many Mexicans had no religious affiliation at all.

Some clergy recognized the Church's need to help improve immigrants' working conditions. For example, there were priests supporting the United Farm Workers Union (UFW), which grew out of the organizing efforts of Cesar Chavez and Dolores Huerta to help Mexicans and Mexican Americans working in the fields of California in the 1960s. With his dramatic fasts and calls to boycott grapes that were not picked by unionized workers, Chavez brought national attention to the plight of agricultural workers and helped the union win early victories. A walk, supported by some priests, from the UFW headquarters in Delano, California, to Sacramento, California's capital, helped secure the passage of a state law that granted agricultural workers the right to form a union. However, from a peak of forty-five thousand union members, the UFW suffered severe losses after the 1970s. By 1984, the UFW had contracts with only fifteen of seventy Delano grape growers. When Chavez died in 1993, the UFW was nearly defunct; in 2007 the federal government reported that the UFW had fewer than six thousand members.

The weakness of the UFW dramatized for Mexican American leaders the importance of political action. The Republicans' strong stand against Cuban dictator Fidel Castro gave them an edge among Cubans and Cuban Americans. But for Mexicans, Castro was hardly a concern. Border issues, good paying jobs, and decent schools in safe neighborhoods were much more important for Mexican Americans. In 2006, the Republican-controlled House of Representatives rejected proposals for an amnesty and for temporary worker programs; favored building additional walls along the border between the United States and Mexico, and made it a crime to assist illegal immigrants. Had such legislation passed, ministers and priests who worked with immigrants would be violating the law.

Such proposals infuriated Mexicans. To have an impact with the state and federal government's political action was needed, and this meant voting. Voting required naturalization but traditionally Mexicans had low rates of naturalization. By 2008 only 21.7 percent of Mexican immigrants had become United States citizens, compared to 42 percent of the foreign-born population overall. Mexico's decision to allow dual citizenship in 1997 also gave Mexican American political leaders

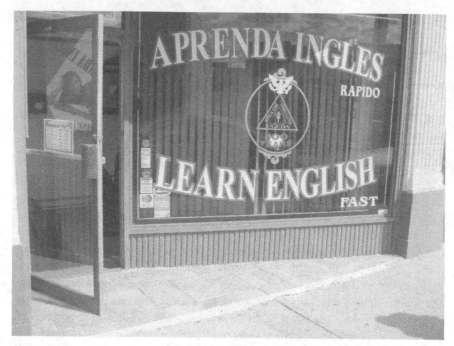

Photo 4-3 English Language Learning Centers Have Spread from California to New York

an argument for encouraging immigrants to naturalize, but Mexicans still lagged behind others in acquiring citizenship. Historically Mexican immigrants had had low rates of naturalization simply because it had been easy to come and go across the border. In addition, so many Mexicans had arrived only recently. A higher fee for the application for citizenship, beginning in mid-2007, was also a deterrent.

Another reason, besides the cost and being close to home, was awareness of American political culture. Iowan Bernard Ortiz, who lived in a state with a growing Mexican population, explained, "Lots of new citizens come here with an old country mentality. They feel their vote doesn't matter and the rich always win." In addition, Ortiz said, "A lot of people are scared to get involved because they think that immigration [ICE] will come for them." Nonetheless, as they became citizens in the 2000s increased percentages of Mexicans began to vote and to make a difference in the outcome of elections. They went overwhelmingly Democratic in 2008, when Barack Obama was elected president, but when they came out in lesser numbers for the congressional elections in 2010, Republicans captured sixty-three new seats in the House of Representatives.

CUBANS

Most Cuban immigrants reached the United States before 1980, but in that year the Mariel Cubans, who numbered 130,000, arrived. Largely single, working-class black men, they had a difficult time adjusting. They were not always welcome even in Miami's large Cuban community because some Cubans believed that they were the product of Castro's communist state and did not fully appreciate political and economic freedom. A few thousand had been criminals in Cuba, and others later committed crimes in the United States and were incarcerated. After much discussion between the US and Cuban governments, Cuba agreed to take back several thousand people. The vast majority of the group, however, avoided conflicts with the law and struggled to maintain themselves. By 2010 most of them had found employment and had integrated themselves within the Cuban American community.

Another group of Cubans, "the rafters," arrived on small boats or rafts in 1994. They numbered only thirty-four thousand, but their presence triggered negotiations between the Clinton administration and Cuba. Castro agreed to stop Cuban citizens from leaving, and the United States arranged to screen Cubans before they left the island, and to concentrate on admitting relatives of those already here along with a few thousand refugees annually. This agreement virtually repealed the Cuban Adjustment Act of 1966 and led to a steady controlled migration of over twenty thousand annually.

In spite of the new agreement, there were still some Cubans who were not included, but they decided to make the journey anyway. Among them were doctors and other medical professionals. From the early days of the 1959 revolution, Cuba had been sending its physicians to other nations in exchange for vital commodities such as oil. In 2006, the Department of Homeland Security began a program that allowed Cuban medical professionals, who had studied or practiced in other nations, to enter the United States legally. About six thousand doctors and other medical providers took advantage of the offer. Once in the United States, however, these immigrants often had difficulty passing licensing exams for their profession. Since they had been paid only about $25 monthly for overseas work by the Cuban government, the newly arrived Cuban physicians who did not qualify to practice medicine in the United States willingly accepted less desirable positions as medical technicians or nurses while again studying for their licensing exams. Miami was said to be "awash" in Cuban doctors, and some of these physicians found other positions. Dr. Carlos Dominguez, a hospice admissions nurse, reportedly earned one hundred thousand dollars annually. He recalled, "I've had to get used to thinking as a nurse, but it's difficult. Deep down, I'm still a doctor."

DOMINICANS

The United States' close ties with the Dominican Republic during the twentieth century helped stimulate immigration. American troops had occupied the Dominican Republic between 1916 and 1924, and American culture has continued to permeate that country ever since. Until the 1965 Hart-Celler Act placed a ceiling on the Western Hemisphere, Dominicans could easily immigrate legally to the United States. However, after 1930, the Dominican Republic's dictator, Rafael

Leonidas Trujillo Molinas discouraged emigration. In addition to living under Trujillo's harsh regime, citizens faced dismal economic conditions. In the year after his 1961 assassination, the number of Dominicans who headed to the United States tripled. It tripled again the next year and almost tripled a third time from 1962 to 1963. In 1965 Americans briefly reoccupied the Dominican Republic to shore up a conservative government. American soldiers left after a few months, but during that time many Dominican urbanites learned of the latest advances in American consumer culture: cars, electronics, and household goods. More Dominicans thought that they, too, should head for the United States, and once remittances began flowing back to the Dominican Republic, residents had the funds to leave the country.

New York City attracted the overwhelming majority of these immigrants, both legal and unauthorized. In 1990 Dominican immigrants outnumbered Italians as the largest foreign-born group in New York, although they remained second in size to Puerto Ricans as the largest Hispanic-born population in the city. However, because so many Dominicans lacked proper documents, demographers claimed that census counts missed many of them.

To earn a living, some Dominicans purchased bodegas, small grocery stores that had been owned by Puerto Ricans before them. Despite long hours and hard work, the new entrepreneurs barely earned enough to maintain a decent lifestyle for their families. The most profitable stores tried to attract customers by offering familiar goods that could not be found in American supermarkets.

Most other Dominicans labored in New York's service industries, cleaning stores and hotels, working as janitors, or driving taxi cabs, all positions that paid low wages. For women, getting away from home and moving into the workforce gave them more freedom than they had had in the Dominican Republic. These women told researchers in the 1980s that they resisted their husbands' desire to go back home. In New York City, they not only went to work, but, unlike in the Dominican Republic, men shared some of the domestic responsibilities because their wives brought home badly needed wages. One immigrant wife told researchers that her husband had learned to cook because if he hadn't he might not eat.

Dominican family life mirrored that of many poor immigrant minorities as well as African Americans. Nearly half of Dominican women immigrants lived without husbands. If they had preschool age children, there was little affordable decent child care, so they often did not seek outside employment and were forced to rely on welfare to make ends meet. Like many immigrants from other countries, thousands of Dominicans believed that their stay in America was temporary. They sent money home to help relatives, and saved in order to buy retirement houses in the Dominican Republic. Those who had legal standing visited relatives in the Dominican Republic as often as they could. Going home for the Christmas holidays was a common experience, especially as air connections became more frequent and less expensive after 1978.

Dominicans began to disperse from New York City and other towns and cities in the 1990s. For those who settled in Providence, Rhode Island, life was little different from New York City. They were less educated than most other residents, and a number were recent arrivals who could not speak English well. As a result their incomes were relatively low; many lived near or in poverty. Their hope was that through education their children would do better economically and would have an improved life.

For those who saw their future in the United States as permanent, political involvement was a draw. In 1994 the Dominican Republic allowed those who lived abroad to retain their citizenship even if they naturalized elsewhere. As other immigrant and ethnic groups had also discovered, political influence was not only important to have better schools and neighborhoods; it also resulted in members of Congress giving serious attention to their concerns.

There was one fairly unique occupational field open to talented young Dominican men: baseball. Many male adolescents and their families believed this was the way to fame and riches. The Dominican Republic sent 444 players to the big leagues after 2001 and had 146 players on Major League Baseball rosters in 2006. Among many stand-outs, Dominican-born players like Albert Pujols of the St. Louis Cardinals and later the Los Angeles Angels and David Ortiz of the Boston Red Sox were the best known. In the 2000s, Dominican young men hoping for a chance to play in the major leagues dominated the roster of the minor league team in Burlington, Vermont. During the winter, Dominican fans living in the Washington Heights neighborhood of New York City watched Dominican teams play on television. One viewer commented, "There is more action in Dominican baseball. Every inning there's a commotion." While watching a championship series in the Dominican Republic, another fan insisted, "For Dominican baseball fans, this is like the Yankees-Red Sox rivalry."

Yet life in America could still be difficult. Washington Heights, the center of Dominican life in New York City, was an area of crime, drug dealing, overcrowded housing, and substandard schools. In 2000, less than one-half of Dominican immigrants had graduated from high school and only 4 percent held college degrees. Another handicap was lack of fluency in English. Most immigrants spoke Spanish; however, their children were learning English and pursuing education further than their parents had. More outrageous for many Dominicans was the racism they encountered if they had a dark skin. Indeed, while these newcomers regarded themselves as Dominicans, some of them were uncertain about where they belonged in the American racial system; were they Hispanics or were they African Americans?

In spite of the hardships encountered in America, migration from the Dominican Republic grew steadily after 1970 and averaged over twenty-five thousand annually. Outside the American embassy in the Dominican Republic, officials faced long lines of those seeking approval of their visa requests to the United States. Immigration from the Dominican Republic dropped, as it did for all nations, in the wake of the terrorist attacks on September 11, 2001, but it picked up again and averaged more than twenty-five thousand per year for the rest of the decade. Its high point occurred in 2011, when 46,109 arrived.

More Dominicans wanted to immigrate, but the new rules of the world-wide preference system limited legal migration. With visas hard to obtain, many Dominicans, like so many Poles, Irish, and Mexicans, came on tourist visas and remained, thus becoming unauthorized immigrants. As a result, American officials eventually began to reject larger numbers of applications for tourist visas. Some Dominicans even went to Puerto Rico first and then flew to the United States, trying to pass as American citizens.

NICARAGUANS

Like Dominicans, Nicaraguans were seeking a better economic life as well as fleeing civil war and violence. Before the 1960s, a few Nicaraguans had come to the United States to escape a reactionary regime led by Anastasio Somoza Garcia's family. When a left-wing government, the Sandinistas, took power in 1979, civil war broke out. The radical Sandinistas soon found themselves facing an insurgent movement supported by the US government. As violence spread, fifteen thousand or so wealthy Nicaraguans fled the country. Most went to Florida, where similarly anticommunist Cubans lived. Thousands of others followed. Nicaraguans often arrived illegally and sought political asylum once in the United States. American courts generally held that fleeing a civil war was insufficient reason to grant asylum, and as a result few Nicaraguans received it. Friends of Nicaraguans pled their cases in the courts and in Congress, arguing that the United States was trying to overthrow a government it considered too radical yet was refusing to grant refugee or asylum status to those persons who were fleeing that same government. Finally, Congress passed the Nicaraguan Adjustment and Central American Relief Act in 1997, and thousands of Nicaraguans who had arrived earlier received an amnesty.

Nicaraguan life centered in Miami, where an estimated one hundred thousand lived by 2008. Anticommunist Cubans assisted the post-1979 initial waves who had fled a radical regime, but because so many of the migrants were without skills and spoke no English, they had to take whatever jobs they could find. Construction work paid best, but opportunities in that industry were scarce. Many Nicaraguans did menial work, and some men stood on street corners with Mexicans and other Hispanics, waiting to be chosen for day jobs. Nicaraguan women obtained employment caring for children and cleaning people's homes.

OTHER CENTRAL AMERICANS

While most Central Americans were similar to Mexicans in education, employment, and English-speaking ability, several differences existed between them and Mexicans. In recent years, a growing number of immigrants from Mexico came from urban areas, but most Guatemalans and Salvadorans were rural in origin.

In addition, some immigrants from Guatemala—for example, Mayans—were not fluent in Spanish or English; instead they spoke only their native Indian languages. On the East Coast, Florida attracted many Guatemalans, mostly Mayan refugees from the Central American wars. Small towns provided a home for agricultural workers who picked Florida's crops. One of the main Florida towns for the Mayans was Indiantown, whose population swelled when citrus fruit needed harvesting. Some of their housing resembled the substandard dwellings of migrant workers during the Great Depression or the days of the Bracero Program.

The largest number of Central Americans hailed from El Salvador. Like Nicaraguans, they too were fleeing civil war. In addition, El Salvador, like other Central American nations, was periodically hit by violent hurricanes, flooding, mudslides, and earthquakes that left thousands homeless. Particularly destructive was an earthquake that struck in 2001. Once in the United States, El Salvadoran undocumented immigrants requested asylum, but the vast majority of pleas was rejected. The administrations of Ronald Reagan and his successor, George H. W. Bush, insisted that these newcomers were economic immigrants and were not entitled to asylum. If these presidents relaxed asylum policy, it would have been an admission that the United States was supporting allied governments that were committing civil and human rights abuses against their own citizens. As a result, in the 1980s only 2 percent of El Salvadorans and Guatemalans received asylum. This figure compares to the roughly 50 percent of Iranians who applied for and received asylum or obtained refugee status in the United States during the same decade. The Nicaraguan and Central American Relief Act provided an amnesty for some Central Americans, but it did not aid those coming after 1997.

The Immigration Reform and Control Act of 1986 was more important in providing amnesty for unauthorized Central American immigrants who arrived before 1982. Mexican immigrants had received the largest number of amnesties granted; the second largest group was the 146,000 given to Salvadoran migrants; and Guatemalans ranked third with 100,000. However, many Central Americans continued to flee after 1986 because their civil wars did not end until the 1990s; Guatemala's peace accord was signed in 1992, and El Salvador's in 1996. Some experts thought that with the end of bloodshed the flow of immigrants would decrease and many Central Americans would return home. However, a large-scale exodus from the United States did not occur. By 2005, over 1.3 million Guatemalans who had left their country after 1960 continued to reside in the United States; the figures from El Salvador were double those from Guatemala. A majority of El Salvadorans and Guatemalans settled in California, Illinois, New York, New Jersey, Texas, and later, Florida. Because immigrant networks guided newcomers to communities comprising their fellow countrymen, such concentrations were not unusual. Like Mexicans, they found employment along the "chicken trail," and often worked in chicken and meat processing plants alongside Mexicans, Hondurans, and other Hispanic immigrants.

AN IMMIGRANT'S TALE

Luisa Rojas, from Guatemala, 1968

Her story reveals the problems of those who come without documents, with poor English, and a lack of skills to obtain a highly paid job. Another important fact of life for immigrants, including those without documents, was contact with people already in the United States.

Seeking a better life, with the help of friends, Luisa Rojas came to the United States and managed to find employment in New York City. But she lacked "papers," meaning legal status, and she struggled with her English. Her great fear was "immigration"—the officials that might come and catch her to deport her. Her constant fear of deportation was real, as a growing number of immigrants are deported each year, reaching about four hundred thousand in 2012. Many of those deported were guilty of serious crimes, but many were also illegal immigrants who were caught by officials and sent packing.

Rojas managed to obtain employment in New York City, but the job was not well paid. But with the help of friends she obtained a social security card, and then a better job in New Jersey. Her good fortune was to work for people who were able to obtain the necessary paperwork for her to become a legal immigrant. When she got to see the lawyer, she was "happy."

SOUTH AMERICANS

Immigration from South America also began to increase after the 1970s. Over one half million South American newcomers arrived in the 1990s, and this influx continued at a steady pace. In the 2000s it averaged about seventy-five thousand annually. It reached 80,096 in 2011. Along with Central Americans and Mexicans, South Americans were part of the growing Latino presence in the United States. However, immigrants from Brazil were Portuguese-speaking, and many of those from Guyana were ethnically Asian Indians, so they stood apart. The largest South American sending nations were Brazil, Colombia, Ecuador, Argentina, and Venezuela. Many of these latest newcomers were undocumented, although not nearly as many as Central Americans and Mexicans. Moreover, the social characteristics of South Americans were quite different from those of Central Americans and Mexicans. Seventy-four percent of South American immigrants were high school graduates, and one-quarter had college degrees. Although 80 percent spoke a language other than English at home, 60 percent of South Americans reported that they spoke English well. In short, South American migrants tended to be middle class, like the Cubans who came shortly after their revolution, from 1960 to 1973.

As a result of the violence that began the 1950s, many Colombians emigrated. They sought peace and better economic conditions. The first wave of emigrants, those who left during the era of "La Violencia," comprised largely middle-class people who ventured to Venezuela and the United States. But violence remained a constant theme in Colombian life. In the 1990s, some experts named Colombia as the most dangerous place in the world. Since the 1990s, in addition to the drug trade, human trafficking increased, with Colombia being the main South American nation involved in the prostitution trade. Young women caught up in this horror were sent primarily to Europe and Asia, but a few also found themselves working as prostitutes in the United States. In 2002 the Colombian government put new measures in place to curb the violence and bring the left-wing Revolutionary Armed Forces of Colombia under control. Despite this effort a senior fellow at the Council of Foreign Relations wrote, "Between drugs, paramilitaries, guerrillas, and a collapsing state, Colombia's condition is steadily worsening."

The violence and the poorly functioning economy stimulated a continuing exodus from Colombia. In the 1990s, government officials had difficulty keeping up with applications for passports. By the 2000s, the United States was admitting roughly 20,000 Colombians per year; the figure was 27,849 in 2009. It dropped slightly to 22,635 in 2011. Most experts believe that a greater number arrived on tourist visas and remained when their permits expired. In recent years, many Colombians settled in South Florida, where so many other Hispanics lived and there was little chance of being deported.

Brazilians also responded to a deteriorating economy by leaving. Those emigrating between the late 1970s and the 2000s were often white, middle-class college graduates, and were not representative of Brazil's population. Settling in Massachusetts and New York, they were emigrating from a nation that was experiencing inflation, high taxes, and a financial crisis. In places like Mount Vernon, New York, they formed vibrant Brazilian communities. Mount Vernon featured Brazilian-owned bars, bakeries, a butcher shop, and restaurants that catered to Brazilian cultural tastes. As the United States economy weakened in 2007 and 2008 and Brazil offered better economic opportunities, some Brazilians who had arrived illegally returned home. One said, "You can't spend your whole life waiting to be legal."

CHAPTER 5

A Record Surge of Immigrants, 1990–2012

Immigration reached a record level between 1990 and 2010 as over twenty million foreigners arrived in the United States. Not since the years 1900–1920, when more than fourteen million arrived, had the nation seen such a large number of newcomers in a twenty-year period. Of the nation's forty million immigrants in 2012, over one-half arrived after 1990. By 2012 the foreign-born population of the United States was nearly 13 percent; it had been less than 5 percent in 1970. An estimated eleven million undocumented newcomers lived in the United States in 2010 and many have been missed in the official accounts. Illegal immigration had been especially heavy from 1995 to 2007, before it declined during the recession that began in 2008. In fact, undocumented arrivals fell by 67 percent between 2000 and 2009 from an average of 850,000 a year to 300,000 annually.

As in the past, six states proved particularly attractive to the newcomers. As Table 5.1 shows, each of them significantly increased the number of their foreign-born between 1990 and 2010, and each received at least two-thirds of a million new immigrants.

Besides large numbers, a second feature of the developing post-1990 immigration system was the dispersal of the new arrivals. They settled in every part of

Table 5.1 Foreign-Born Population

STATE	1990	2006	2009
California	6,458,825	8,864,255	9,946,758
New York	2,851,861	3,864,255	4,178,170
Texas	1,524,436	2,899,642	3,985,239
Florida	1,662,601	2,670,828	3,484,141
New Jersey	966,610	1,476,327	1,759,467
Illinois	952,272	1,529,058	1,740,763

SOURCE: Department of Homeland Security (DHS), *Statistical Yearbook*, 2010.

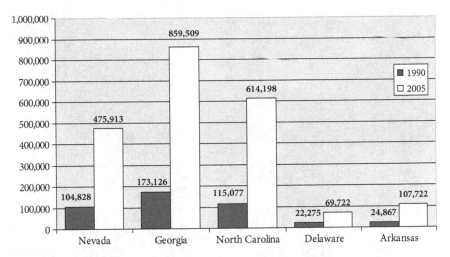

Figure 5.1 Foreign-Born Population
SOURCE: DHS, *Statistical Yearbook*, 2006.

the nation, and their impact was felt in urban, rural, and suburban areas. As the figure above illustrates, states that had seen relatively few immigrants before experienced significant growth in their foreign-born populations.

Finally it should be noted that after 1990 a majority of newcomers settled in suburbs. A huge exodus from the cities occurred after 1945, as jobs and people fled cramped urban dwellings for greener pastures elsewhere. This movement took place in the rings of settlements near both large and small cities. As the American economy changed from a post-1945 industrial base to a service oriented one, the best jobs were more apt to be further away from downtown areas. Immigrants knew where they wanted to go. After 1990 they, especially the highly educated professionals, settled where jobs, and quality schools for their children, were located. As an immigration think tank expert put it, "Immigrants have followed the suburban job and housing opportunities in great numbers. By doing so they have broken historical patterns of immigrants moving to cities where housing and jobs were plentiful and where they found others from their own background. Now many immigrants move directly to suburban areas from abroad."

A prototype for the changes can be seen in the city and environs of Philadelphia. From 1950 through 1970 the foreign-born population remained around 250,000, and then it began to grow. Today two-thirds of the immigrants in the Philadelphia area have been in the United States for twenty years or less, and one-third came only in the last decade. In 2010 the area housed over half a million foreigners. In 1970, about half of the newcomers lived in the city and the other half lived in the suburbs. By 2010 over 70 percent resided in the suburbs. And, like the national trend, 80 percent of Philadelphia's immigrants in 1970 hailed from Europe; in 2010 only 23 percent of them were born in Europe, while 39 percent came from Asia and 28 percent from Latin America. The top three foreign groups living in

Photo 5-1 The Foreign Language Press Has Expanded with the Increase in Immigration

the city in 2010 were from India, China, and Vietnam; in the metropolitan area, however, Mexicans ranked third behind the Chinese and the Indians. In terms of education the immigrants are at both extremes. They are more likely than other Philadelphians to have a B.A. or higher degree, but some never completed high school. About one-third of the newcomers speak English well; another 43 percent have difficulty with the language. These and similar patterns will be seen among the various groups discussed in this chapter.

BACKGROUND

Why did a massive movement of peoples in the late twentieth century occur? One important reason for the post-1990 mass immigration was the change in American immigration laws. The Immigration Reform and Control Act (IRCA) of 1986 gave an amnesty to nearly three million people, but the paper work delayed a change in status until after 1989, and those receiving the amnesty (and many of their family members) were mostly recorded in the 1990s. In 1991 the Immigration and Naturalization Service (INS) counted 1.8 million new immigrants, the highest one-year figure in American history, but roughly half had received IRCA amnesties. Moreover, the Immigration Act of 1990 increased immigration 35 percent. Among the changes was a more flexible limit for the country quotas. Business groups wanting highly educated immigrants succeeded in persuading Congress to increase the number of places up to 140,000 annually for skilled workers. The act also created a category for diversity visas that eventually numbered fifty thousand annually. Several limited amnesties in the 1990s for Central Americans and Haitians also enabled persons to become refugees and then immigrants.

The end of colonialism continued to have an impact on the movement of people from Asia and Africa, as did the establishment of American military bases throughout the world. These factors help to account for immigration from India and more recently from Pakistan and Bangladesh. In 1917 Congress barred Indians from entrance to the United States. Great Britain granted independence for India and Pakistan in 1946, but the United States granted the new countries only minimum quotas of one hundred per year until passage of the Hart-Celler Act of 1965. Bangladesh achieved independence from Pakistan in 1971 and received twenty-thousand quota slots per year as provided in the Immigration Act of 1965. Indian immigration began to grow in the 1980s, while that of Pakistan and Bangladesh increased later; in 2009 these three nations collectively sent nearly one hundred thousand immigrants to the United States. President Richard Nixon visited China in 1972, and this and other events helped to open immigration from China. Chinese immigration further increased in the 1980s, and after 1990 the Chinese became one of the leading groups of newcomers entering the United States.

When the national origins quotas became effective in the 1920s, only a few independent African nations, such as Ethiopia, had quotas, and these were only the one hundred minimum allotted to countries that had sent small numbers of free persons to the United States before that decade. From 1920 to 1970 only forty thousand Africans were recorded as immigrants. The Diversity Visa (DV) created by the Immigration Act of 1990 enabled many Africans to immigrate to the United States. If a nation sent fewer than fifty thousand immigrants to the United States over the previous five years then persons from that country were eligible for the DVs, which were distributed via a lottery. No nation was to receive more than thirty-eight hundred DVs annually. Once the DV became part of the immigration process, each year millions of persons applied for these lottery slots.

The transportation and technological revolutions of the post-1960 world also played a role in the massive movement of people. With the advent of jet travel, immigrants could reach their destinations in a matter of hours, not days. Before 1920 a journey from India or China to the United States cost a great deal of money and took weeks to accomplish. In the 1990s the trip from Asia to the United States could be done in hours, and emigrants often found bargain air fares to make the trip affordable. The Internet made it possible to maintain contact with the homeland and people left behind, and the modern methods of transfers of money made the sending of remittances easy.

Certainly, civil wars, health concerns, and economics also played important roles. Global economic integration and the expansion of the American economy attracted immigrants who sought opportunities not available in their own nations. Undocumented immigration to the United States dipped because of the economic downturn in late 2007, but the demand for immigrant visas to America remained strong. A huge backlog of people waited to use the existing preference systems in the American immigration laws. Thus if some persons chose not to emigrate, others took their places.

AFRICANS

Except for South Africans, most Americans had not seen many immigrants from south of the Saharan Desert since the days of the slave trade. The largest northern African sending nation was Egypt. Before 1970 many of the Sub-Saharan Africans who came to the United States arrived on student visas rather than as regular immigrants. In the 1980s the number of African immigrants doubled, and in the 1990s doubled again. The Bureau of the Census counted nearly one million African-born persons in 2000. After the census this migration continued to grow. In 2001, 50,009 immigrants from Africa were recorded, more than twice the figure of 1989. African immigration to the United States topped 127,000 in 2009, which was 11 percent of all immigrants that year and greater than the number of Europeans arriving. By 2009, the African community in the United States numbered 1.5 million compared to only 35,000 in 1970, and constituted nearly 4 percent of the entire immigrant population. Some authorities believe that blacks constituted only 60 percent of Africans counted in the 1990 census of the United States. The proportion of black Africans increased after that date, and in 2012 it was estimated 1.1 million of Africans were black. It is important to point out that African emigrants included both white and black persons. Much of the exodus occurred because many people rejected the Apartheid policies of South Africa or feared that the newly independent nations would persecute whites. Also included among African immigrants were Asians, the descendants of immigrants from India who had been recruited in the nineteenth century to work in Africa, largely as builders of railroads. These Asian Africans accounted for about 10 percent of African immigrants in the United States in 1990.

Although the colonial era began to crumble in Africa after World War II, the continent continued to be plagued by major problems. The Europeans who had governed different colonies had not prepared the indigenous people to assume the reigns of government and steer the economy. Moreover, the Europeans had never fostered quality education for the Africans, although some of them journeyed to cities like Amsterdam, Brussels, Paris, Lisbon, and London for advanced studies. Civil wars and violence were common in many of the newly independent nations, often among tribes whose organizations transcended national boundaries. The 1994 genocide in Rwanda was perhaps the most outstanding example of the continent's violence. A chilling 2008 report by Doctors Without Borders revealed that thousands from Chad were fleeing their homeland; postelection upheavals left many dead in Kenya that year; and violence was continuing in the Democratic Republic of the Congo. Moreover, Africa has experienced droughts and the AIDS epidemic, and malaria was killing children in Sierra Leone. By the 1990s the existing turmoil left Africa with the largest number of refugees on the world's continents.

AN IMMIGRANT'S TALE

Lopez Lomong was born in war-torn East Africa, a place of violence and destruction accompanying the war in Sudan. Eventually two million died and thousands of children were enslaved. When, at age six, he and other children found themselves under attack in their village, Lomong fled. Because he could not be found, his parents believed that he was dead and actually held a funeral for him. He became one of the "Lost Boys of Sudan," the young men and boys who lived in Sudan's refugee camps, their survival and whereabouts unknown to their families. After ten years in his camp, he learned that the United States was going to admit several thousand "Lost Boys" as refugees.

Beginning a new life in the United States in 2000 in upstate New York, he had major adjustments to make and unfamiliar practices to learn. On his first night in the United States he slept with the light on: he did not know how to turn it off. Nor did he realize that the shower could be regulated between hot and cold. "I was shivering so hard. I thought that's how white people get white, they shower in cold water."

While in high school he demonstrated that he was a good runner, and became a New York state champion in the 1,500-meter race. While attending Northern Arizona State University, Lomong became a champion college runner, and after becoming a US citizen in the summer of 2008, he qualified for the US Olympic team. "Before, I ran from danger and death," he declared. "Now, I run for sport. It would be an honor to represent the country that saved me and showed me the way." He carried the American flag for the US athletes at the opening ceremony. Lomong was not alone: the United States was represented by thirty-two foreign-born athletes in the 2008 Olympic Games.

It was not simply the poor who experienced hardship; many African professionals who were seeking higher wages, political stability, and improved working facilities, went to the countries that had colonized them (Great Britain, the Netherlands, France, and Portugal) in the late nineteenth century. When the receiving European nations became less welcoming to their former colonists, the United States appeared attractive, especially as America's immigration laws became more inviting. Roughly one-half of the African migrants who listed an occupation reported that they were in professional, managerial, and technical categories.

African students stood in the vanguard of this wave of increased immigration to the United States. This mirrored the pattern established by Asians from the Philippines, Korea, Taiwan, China, and India in the 1980s. After completing their studies many students chose to remain in the United States. They adjusted from student to immigrant status, found employment, and/or married Americans. From 1978 to 1989 roughly twenty-six hundred African students annually adjusted their status, which accounted for 15 percent of immigrants from Africa. The majority of these immigrants were men, as were the majority of African immigrants generally, which is somewhat different from the flow of immigrants to America between 1945 and 2012, when a slight majority of all immigrants were women.

Some African nations regretted that so many students failed to return home, a concern shared by Europeans in the immediate postwar era of a "brain drain" to the United States. For example, one study revealed that 35 percent of Ethiopian students sent abroad remained in the countries where they had pursued their advanced educations. Another study found similar figures, and reported that 43 percent of women remained in the countries where they had completed their education. During the 1980s and 1990s, Kenya, Nigeria, Ghana, Egypt, and South Africa furnished the largest number of students who went to Europe or the United States.

Engineers, college professors, doctors, nurses, and economists abounded among the highly educated Africans who emigrated after 1990. In 2006, Ethiopia had only one full-time economics professor, but there were one hundred Ethiopian economists in the United States. While the migration of those with Ph.D.s concerned many African officials, it was the emigration of medical professionals that drew the most attention. Most foreign-born nurses in the United States were Filipinas, but some African women also found employment in American hospitals. The flight of doctors was even more critical for African nations facing severe health problems. Sixty percent of Ghanaian-trained physicians reportedly left during the 1980s. Thus it is no surprise that statistics describing Africans in America showed high levels of education. The 1990 census and other data revealed that among African immigrants 47 percent had graduated from college, and 22 percent held graduate degrees. These levels were higher than for some Asian immigrants. The exodus of well-educated Africans continued after 1990, and in 2007 40 percent of African adults in the United States held a bachelor's degree or higher, compared to one-quarter of native-born Americans who were college graduates. Once in the United States, Africans had to compete with Asians and other highly educated immigrant groups for desirable positions. But now the "brain drain" included Africa as well as Asia.

The flow of African refugees to the United States also continued in the 1990s and 2000s. When a leftist government took control of Ethiopia during the 1970s, the United States admitted a few thousand Ethiopians as its first African refugee group. In the 1970s and 1980s, America took in 24,030 African refugees, 19,849 of them from Ethiopia. With the end of the Cold War, American refugee policy shifted from an anticommunist base to a more humanitarian one. In the early 1990s, a civil war broke out in Somalia. As a result of this conflagration a new refugee process developed, with Somalis dominating the flow after 2000. In 2004, 13,331 Somalis entered the United States as refugees; 10,405 followed the next year; and in 2010 census takers counted 85,700 of them in the country, about 25,000 in

Photo 5-2 African Refugees Have Settled Throughout the United States. This Center is in Vermont

Minnesota. Some of these newcomers were the "lost boys of Sudan" described above, who had lived for years in refugee camps.

Africans also benefited from the lottery that was written into the Immigration Act of 1990. The United States gave Africans twenty thousand of the fifty thousand yearly DV slots although the actual number arriving varied. These rules clearly aided Africans because, as a group, they accounted for slightly less than 4 percent of America's foreign-born but received 40 percent of the new lottery visas. In 2009, more than fourteen thousand lottery places went to Africans. For example, Nigerians received 3,720; Egyptians, 3,336; Ethiopians, 3,829; Kenyans, 2,324; and Moroccans, 2,100.

The United States also received a large number of undocumented African immigrants. During the 1970s, a growing number of Senegalese began to appear on New York City's streets selling trinkets and inexpensive goods to passers-by. On rainy days they sold umbrellas, but on other days, their stock included baseball caps, books, watches, cheap jewelry, and a variety of electronic goods. By the 1980s, African street merchants, who were overwhelmingly men, also sold their wares in other American cities. But unauthorized Africans also performed a variety of other jobs as well. For example, undocumented African delivery men, who earned only two dollars per hour for lugging bags of groceries to New York City's apartments, sued the food chain Food Emporium for paying less than the minimum wage. They won their case. The plight of undocumented Africans who came before 1982 was eased by the 1986 amnesty; over thirty thousand of them were able to legalize their status.

Whether they arrived as students, well-educated professionals, or refugees, with visas obtained by the lottery, or simply as unauthorized immigrants, the new Africans were forming a network facilitating immigration to the United States. Once they obtained a green card, which allowed them to work legally in the United States, they used the preference system for families to join them. Those who became US citizens could sponsor immediate family members (spouses, children, and parents) over the quota. In 2005, for example, of the 85,102 Africans admitted in that year, 4,387 were family-sponsored immigrants under the preferences, and 29,039 were immediate family members of US citizens and thus exempt from the quotas. These relatives of US citizens accounted for about one-third of the total that year.

According to the 2000 census New York City housed about one hundred thousand Africans, the largest concentration in the nation. Because of the continued flow since then, and the presence of many undocumented African immigrants during the past decade, by 2010 the actual figure was larger and estimated to be 125,000. The city's Africans included Nigerian physicians and refugees from Liberia, along with many undocumented migrants from Senegal.

In terms of impact, the Washington, DC, African immigrant community stands out. In 2000, 93,271 Africans constituted over 11 percent of the metropolitan area's population. Africans have also scattered throughout the United States. In part this pattern was due to refugees who were settled by the federal government in collaboration with state and voluntary organizations. A particularly active program in Minneapolis accounts for so many Somalis living in Minnesota. Other places where African immigrants have settled are St. Louis, Grand Rapids, and Seattle. Even Tucson, Arizona, known for its large Hispanic population, housed several hundred African immigrant families. States with colder climates, like Vermont and Colorado, reported smaller numbers of African immigrants. Africans living along Colorado's ski slopes were reported to be undocumented workers who wintered in the area. Refugees also found homes in Lewiston, Maine, where they were met with a frigid welcome. After the initial tension between the Lewiston residents and the refugees, a peace prevailed when a number of Africans left the community.

HAITIANS

After the 1980s other black immigrants besides Africans increased their migration to the United States. Jamaican and Haitian immigrants averaged over twenty thousand annually from 2000 to 2006. Jamaicans alone numbered nearly 21,783 in 2009 and fell slightly to 19,662 in 2011. For the people of Haiti dreadful economic and political conditions continued even after the regime of a dictatorial regime ended in the late 1970s. Haiti was plagued with poverty, violence, and constant political turmoil. Haitians arriving before 1982 received an amnesty under IRCA,

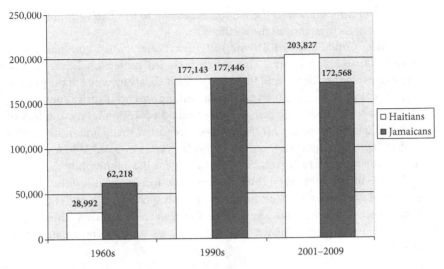

Figure 5.2 Immigration from Haiti and Jamaica
SOURCE: DHS, *Statistical Yearbook*, 2009.

but for those entering illegally, or legally, life was hard. Bill Clinton had criticized President Ronald Reagan's policy of intercepting Haitian illegal "boat people" and sending them to America's Guantanamo base in Cuba, but as President Clinton followed the same policy.

In 1994, President Clinton sent American military forces to Haiti in an attempt to restore order and democracy to the country and stem a flood of poor Haitian immigrants to the United States. Clinton insisted that if order were not restored, the United States would be faced with an invasion of "boat people" from Haiti. Toward the end of Clinton's term in office, Congressional supporters of Haitians passed the Haitian Fairness Refugee Act of 1999, which established procedures that permitted over twenty thousand Haitians to receive asylum. Moreover, enough Haitians had become immigrants by the 1990s that they were able to sponsor their relatives under the family unification sections of the immigration law. In 2006, for example, of Haiti's 22,228 immigrants, 3,624 came under the family preferences; 8,937 were immediate family members of United States citizens; and 6,101 were granted asylum or came as refugees. However, those who could not gain legal entry or status in the United States continued to flee their homeland by boat. In January 2009, the Coast Guard intercepted 624 Haitians at sea and sent them home. Weeks later nine Haitians drowned at sea before the Coast Guard found them. In 2010, a massive earthquake devastated Haiti, killing three hundred thousand people, orphaning thousands, and leaving one million families homeless. The US government offered undocumented Haitians the right to remain in the country, at least until conditions improved. Moreover, the United States sent millions of aid dollars to that shattered country. How long it would take Haiti to return to normal was anybody's guess in 2010, but "normal" for Haitians usually meant a high rate of poverty, thus a key driver of immigration to the United States would not likely diminish even after the nation recovered from the earthquake.

By 2010, a middle class had emerged among the Haitian communities of New York, Boston, and Miami. This group included professionals, merchants, and service personnel. But overall these newcomers constituted one of the poorest immigrant communities in America. Such a ranking was no surprise considering the health of many when they arrived, their limited education levels, and lack of English language proficiency. Moreover, it was reported that some of those who arrived as legal immigrants looked down on the "boat people." When Haitians celebrated their culture in organizations and everyday life, many whites, and even some blacks, insisted that they should acculturate to American values and not perpetuate Haitian ones. Light-skinned people who spoke French rather than the Haitian dialect were sometimes unwilling to accept the new Haitians. Those arriving in Miami encountered Cubans who were not eager to offer them much assistance either.

MIDDLE EASTERNERS

Near Easterners or Middle Easterners, as some were referred to, had been coming to the United States since the end of World War II, but their numbers grew substantially after the 1980s. American Arab and non-Arab communities already established in the country offered a familiar place for the latest newcomers from Egypt, Israel, Jordan, and Syria after 1990. Earlier immigrants from these lands sent news of the United States home and sometimes provided the funds and family connections to facilitate immigration to the United States. These contacts became increasingly important as air transportation made it easier and cheaper to emigrate. Those communities, such as Iranian and Afghan, built on a refugee base, were especially likely to expand. The Iranian population, for example was estimated to be over 250,000 by 2010. The number of students dropped radically after the crisis of 1979 to 1981 when the Iranian government held over fifty American embassy workers hostage and would not allow students to leave the country, but in spite of the conflict between Iran and the United States, several thousand students annually wanted to pursue an American education.

In 2009–2010, 3,533 Iranians were enrolled in American colleges and universities, about one-tenth the number that had been going to school on the eve of the hostage crisis. Since well-educated people in Iran were taught English at school, students who reached the United States faced few problems handling assignments. The barrier to studying in the United States was created by the political situation and security regulations. These Iranian students wanted the training they believed could only be obtained in the United States. As one student at the University of California put it, "In specific areas like engineering, the best schools in the whole world are in the U.S." He concluded, "If you're a good student, there is no reason wasting your time being in other schools."

Yet it was the troubles of Iraq that led to a new flow of refugees. Kurds, whether living in Iraq or Turkey, fought against their governments and prompted some to migrate from those nations. During the 1980s Iran and Iraq fought an eight-year war that took over a million lives. Iraq's dictator, Saddam Hussein, used poison gas against Iran and against the Kurds. The first Gulf War in 1991, between the United States and Iraq, was sparked by Hussein's invasion of oil-rich Kuwait, which temporarily disrupted the nation's oil fields. A coalition of European powers, the United States, Japan, and a few Middle East nations, spearheaded by President George H. W. Bush, quickly expelled the Iraqi army, but then the American president decided to halt the military at the Iraqi border and called on the people there to overthrow the regime of Saddam Hussein. Some attempted to do so, but Hussein quickly crushed the rebellion while killing thousands of rebels. In the northern part of the country Hussein attacked Kurds, but the United States quickly established a "no fly zone" that prevented Hussein from accomplishing his goal of controlling the Kurds. Following the uprisings and the end of the first Gulf War, about sixteen thousand Iraqis were accepted in the United States, most admitted as refugees. One Iraq group, Chaldean Christians, had established a community in the Detroit area before World War II, and others joined them after 1990.

The second Gulf War began in 2003 when the United States invaded Iraq. As a result of the invasion, as many as two million Iraqis fled to neighboring Jordan and Syria, with a similar number losing their homes in Iraq. Throughout the world most refugees have lived through horrendous, often violent, experiences, and the Iraqis who fled their country in 2003 and after also faced difficult times. When the United States invaded Iraq, President George W. Bush claimed that the war would end quickly with an American victory and a new democratic nation. But the war did not end quickly, the conflagration witnessed increasingly violent struggles, and "democracy" has yet to be demonstrated in Iraq.

Unfortunately for Iraq these refugees were the very people who were badly needed at home. They included doctors, nurses, teachers, and educated persons with the technical skills required to rebuild the country. They also included Christians, who were facing persecution by some of Iraq's radical Islamic groups. By 2007, both Syria and Jordan began to restrict the number of refugees seeking asylum. In addition to those who fled, authorities estimated that another two million persons were displaced from their homes in Iraq. The Bush administration paid little attention to those uprooted by the war; indeed, in 2007 one small city in Sweden took in more refugees than did the United States. Refugee relief organizations, church groups, the United Nations, and Democratic politicians urged the administration to accept more refugees and help those without homes in Iraq. In response, the federal government announced in July 2008 that the United States would initiate a more generous admissions policy, but the process was slow and only twelve thousand Iraqis were accepted that year and another seventeen thousand came in 2009. John Bolton, President Bush's ambassador to the United Nations, declared that the Iraqi refugees have "absolutely nothing to do with our overthrow of Saddam. Our obligation was to give them new institutions and provide security. We have fulfilled that obligation. I don't think we have an obligation to compensate them for the hardships of war." However, Iraqis have continued to arrive in 2010 and 2011. In 2011 21,133 arrived.

AN IMMIGRANT'S TALE

Uday Hatten al-Ghanimi was running a store outside an American base shortly after the invasion of Iraq by the United States began. He was accused by gunmen of being in league with the Americans, and one shot him in the head with a pistol. Severely wounded, Al-Ghanimi underwent several major surgeries to restore his face. As did a number of others from Iraq, he applied for and received political asylum in the United States, but he was one of the few from that troubled land to obtain asylum in the early years of the war. He then petitioned to have his wife and children join him. They did so in July 2009.

New York City often prided itself as home to millions of immigrants and welcoming their diverse cultures and talent. But life was not easy in New York. He had a sense of isolation and inability to work. Al-Ghanimi had a new face, but the pain as a result of his wounds was constant. Unable to work, this fifty-year-old Iraqi refugee was reduced to living on a monthly disability check and food stamps with occasional help from friends. With little income, the family was forced to live in one room in costly New York City. The family's position was aggravated by the fact that his wife and children could not speak English, so they too were isolated from the city's citizens, and were unable to find employment. Al-Ghanimi was not unique among Iraqi refugees. Representatives of international refugee organizations said that they have never seen a group where trauma was so common.

After the destruction of New York City's World Trade Center in 2001 many Americans feared Arabs, became uneasy about Muslims, and opposed bringing Middle Easterners to the United States. As a result Attorney General John Ashcroft ordered the Justice Department to round up and question thousands of young men in the United States who were born in North Africa and the Middle East and deported over one thousand. Using or misusing executive powers and the 2001 Patriot Act, the government watched mosques and arrested several hundred Arabs, whom they held behind bars for months without a hearing. In the next eight years few of these persons were found to be linked in any way to Al Qaeda, the terrorist group responsible for the attacks on the World Trade Center and the Pentagon on September 11, 2001. The American government also froze the assets of several Islamic charities that were alleged to funnel funds to support terrorism. Several older, more established, Muslim charities increased funding for their activities to make up for the loss of funds from other groups.

At the individual level, one man, claiming he was a real "American," killed an Indian Sikh, mistaking him for an Arab. He did not realize that Sikhs wore

Photo 5-3 The Increase of Muslims in America is Illustrated by this Mosque, One of about 2,000 in the United States

turbans. In 2006, a Jet Blue Airline flight attendant ordered an Iraqi-born resident to cover his t-shirt because it had both English and Arabic script saying, "We will not be silent." The man at first resisted the suggestion but later sued the airline and won a $240,000 settlement.

FILIPINOS, SOUTH KOREANS, VIETNAMESE, TAIWANESE, AND CHINESE FROM HONG KONG

Filipinos constitute the nation's largest group of immigrants from any single Asian country after 1990. While immigration from Taiwan, Hong Kong, and even Korea declined, the people of the Philippines continued to arrive because of limited economic opportunities at home. Immigration from the Philippines ran approximately fifty thousand annually. This remained a migration of the well educated, in addition to many poor people who benefited from the family unification preferences. The importance of remittances played a role in this migration, but so did unemployment at home. The world recession in housing and bank failures in 2008 did not thwart the Filipino exodus.

In 2010, one-quarter of Filipino workers were employed in other countries. This included nearly all categories of the occupational scale: maids, nurses, doctors, female welders, computer experts, and seafarers. Indeed, the government established special training centers to provide Filipinos with the skills needed for overseas employment. The centers often taught foreign languages such as Arabic, Cantonese, and Italian. Filipinos were glad to receive training because as one of them noted, "Life in the Philippines is tough." Parts of the Middle East did not experience the recession, and these countries remained attractive for job-seekers.

Filipinos who wanted to immigrate to America faced the backlogs of the preference system. By 2010, over three million people were on a list waiting to be admitted to the United States. Although Congress had raised the national annual quota from 20,000 to 25,620 in 2009, this constituted only a minor change. The most popular preference, for brothers and sisters of US citizens, had a waiting list of over 1.6 million. With the annual number permitting only sixty-five thousand places in the world, the wait could be many years, and in the case of the Filipinos it was over fourteen years. It was still longer for American citizens to bring over their adult children. One Filipino veteran, Pedro Alpay who fought with the Americans in the Philippines during World War II, did not become a citizen until 1992. Because his children were over twenty-one they had to wait fifteen years to join him.

Similar delays plagued both Mexicans and Chinese. Some officials insisted that this wait encouraged persons to enter the United States as visitors and remain when their visas expired. In 2010, there were an estimated 325,000 undocumented men and women from the Philippines in the United States. Such a wait also explains why so many Filipinas used the Internet to seek American citizen husbands.

Immigration from Korea decreased in the 1990s, although it again increased slightly after 2000. Although Korean communities may be found throughout the United States, they are still concentrated in three large metropolitan areas: Los Angeles, New York, and Chicago. In both New York and California, customer-proprietor relations between Koreans and blacks sometimes resulted in conflicts. Store owners experienced hostility from African Americans, who complained of high prices, rudeness, and refusal to employ any of them. On several occasions boycotts occurred and some even became violent.

In 1992, a totally unrelated event, which would have severe consequences for many Koreans, involved four white Los Angeles policemen who were charged with beating a black man in the street. The incident had been caught on tape by a witness and was played on television screens throughout the world. The policemen were arrested and then put on trial. After listening to the evidence presented, the jury concluded that the accused police were not guilty. African Americans, and many other people as well, were outraged by the verdict, and riots broke out in black sections of Los Angeles. Hundreds of Korean merchants in African American areas were victimized, their enterprises destroyed by people from their neighborhoods. The devastation was shocking, and many Koreans believed that the riot "changed everything." Not only did thousands return to their native land after this, but others in Korea also lost their desire to seek new lives in the United States. However, after 2000 Korean immigration increased again and numbered over 22,000 in 2011.

The Vietnamese community in the United States continued to grow after 1990 and over one half million arrived by 2010. The United States and Vietnam had made an arrangement to help bring Vietnamese to America and, as a result, fewer of them came as refugees. Most of the twenty-five thousand Vietnamese who arrived annually came under the family provisions of the Hart-Celler Act. Refugees still arrived from holding camps in Thailand, but international cooperation in the1990s finally led to closing the camps and settling their inhabitants abroad. Some had spent several years in Vietnamese communist centers that tried to "reeducate" them. For these persons, life in Vietnam was cruel, and they wanted to join those who had already gone to America.

The latest newcomers generally settled in existing Vietnamese communities, especially in California. Some of those who had arrived earlier had achieved middle-class status and were able to sponsor their relatives. Many of the immigrants who had formerly been among the elite of Vietnamese society also succeeded economically in the United States. Some of them returned to visit their former homes abroad, and while visiting a few looked for investments and trade possibilities that might be developed between the United States and Vietnam.

Although many of the Asians did well in the United States, most Asian refugees had lower than average American incomes and women fared less well than men. For example, one immigrant niche favored by Vietnamese women was in nail salons. After 1990, many Vietnamese women who worked as manicurists replaced Koreans who had held that occupation before them but who then had moved on to better jobs. The Vietnamese women often worked ten hours a day and earned only 150 dollars per week. With their limited English, such employment was one of the few places where they could find work.

By 2009, immigration from Hong Kong and Taiwan had dropped dramatically. That year fewer than fifteen thousand persons from these two areas arrived as immigrants. Indeed, the number was so low that Taiwan became eligible for the Diversity Visas, and in 2009 eighty-one Taiwanese won the lottery. Opportunities for professionals in Taiwan that had not existed in the early 1980s developed after 2000. By the twenty-first century most were ensconced in their Taiwanese homes and saw no reason to return to or go to America. In the late 1990s Great Britain had ceded Hong Kong to the mainland Chinese government and set aside sixty thousand places for the Chinese who wanted to leave Hong Kong when the Peoples Republic of China (PRC) assumed control, but relatively few accepted that opportunity. Some Chinese settled in Great Britain, while a few thousand Hong Kong Chinese migrated to Canada and established new homes and businesses in the western province of British Columbia, especially the city of Vancouver. And about three or four thousand headed for the United States annually.

PEOPLE'S REPUBLIC OF CHINA

In 1979 President Jimmy Carter announced that the United States would establish diplomatic relations with the People's Republic of China (PRC), and the

United States ceased the fiction that Taiwan was the legitimate government on the mainland. Once that occurred, immigration from the PRC grew dramatically. In 1981 the United States gave both Taiwan and the PRC immigration quotas. Not only did the United States and the PRC establish diplomatic relations, but in the 1970s Chinese universities also began to open their doors for new students through competitive examinations, and permit them to go overseas for additional education. Thousands of well-educated and sophisticated Chinese who had been sent to the countryside for "reeducation" in menial jobs now had a future other than feeding pigs and chickens, tending crops, and dwelling under the most primitive conditions. One young woman, who had been sent to the countryside, later said, "If you asked me to go living that kind of life, I would rather die." Now the Chinese could also look to America to further their studies, and many of these students became the vanguard of immigration to America.

It must also be noted that, because numerical limits existed in immigration law, some Chinese snuck into the United States without appropriate documents. In June 1993, *The Golden Venture*, a Chinese freight ship, ran aground off the coast of Long Island, New York. Authorities discovered that its cargo consisted of illegal aliens from the province of Fujian. These would-be migrants had paid up to thirty thousand dollars each to be brought into the United States by smugglers called "Snakeheads." Once in the United States, many undocumented immigrants were trapped into low-paying jobs as they tried to pay off the smugglers' fees. No one knew how many Chinese immigrants entered illegally, but the federal government estimated their number to be approximately two hundred thousand in 2006.

An incident in Beijing's Tiananmen Square occurred in June 1989 and threatened to curtail the movement of bright Chinese who wished to study for advanced degrees in other countries. Thousands of Chinese students protested the dictatorial nature of the national government and demanded immediate democratic reforms. The event went on for days and was televised to millions of viewers throughout the world. The pictures showed the Chinese government in an unfavorable light, especially after troops were brought in to squash the protest. Many people, both in and outside of China, feared that the uprisings would lead to the end of students as well as immigrants being able to leave the country to study abroad. Although this did not happen, the events that occurred in Tiananmen Square frightened Chinese students living abroad. They feared returning home because they, too, sided with the protesters who opposed their government's tyrannical policies.

Responding to the harsh treatment of the protesters, the US Congress passed a bill in 1992 that allowed 48,211 Chinese students already in the country to remain permanently. President George H. W. Bush signed the new legislation that not only benefited those already in America but that also acted as a stimulant for thousands of other Chinese to apply for admission to American universities. Between 1978 and 2003, in fact, almost four hundred thousand Chinese students arrived in the United States, and after graduation many applied to change their status from student to immigrant, a practice common among many foreign students after they finished their studies. In 2006, the Chinese ranked as the third-largest group of foreign students and scholars in America; and in the academic year 2009–2010 China became the leading source for foreign students. China sent 128,000 students to the United States in that year, which topped India's 104,897. The total for all foreign students in academic year 2009–2010 year numbered 671,616. Young adults were even branching out beyond science, computer technology, and engineering and taking courses in the humanities. One commentator noted, "There's a book getting huge play in China right now explaining liberal arts education."

There is no question that the United States benefited enormously from the knowledge accumulated by the students, especially those who remained afterward. While a number of these individuals distinguished themselves in art, music, film, and literature, most of the Asian graduates entered the fields of scientific research, engineering, computers, and technology.

ASIAN INDIANS

In 2010, there were more than 1.7 million persons of Indian birth in the United States. The actual number of Indian immigrants in the United States is larger than official figures, not because many entered without documents, but because a proportion of immigrants from Trinidad and Guyana, descendants of plantation workers recruited by Great Britain in the nineteenth century, were also Indian in origin. The census reported in 2006 that just over 4 percent of Indians acknowledged that they were born in Guyana, although immigration authorities reported them as natives of Guyana. Several thousand ethnic Indians who had maintained small shops in several African countries also migrated when they were forced out or were fearful of their futures as African colonies became independent. Many of them came to the United States as well. America was not the only land of choice of Indian immigrants. In the decades after India achieved independence from the British in 1946, eighteen million people emigrated from India in search of better opportunities in other lands. The peak year for Indian migration to the United States was 2005 when 79,140 arrived.

The number of immigrants from India grew rapidly after 1990, and among these newcomers were well-educated professionals. A government report published in February 2009 stated that 74 percent of Indians arrived in the United States with bachelor's degrees; almost half had postgraduate educations. Thus Asian Indians who entered the United States after 1946 were well educated and, as a group, had achieved the highest levels of learning. In 2009, they also had one of the highest annual median family incomes in the United States; at $91,195 it was nearly double that of Americans generally.

Medicine, more than any other profession, had a particular attraction for Asian Indians. Since the 1960s the numbers of both medical students and established physicians have shown significant growth. "Go to any hospital in the United States," Dr. Pradeep Tapaar remarked, "and you'll find Indian doctors on the staff." Indian doctors were estimated to number thirty-five thousand by 2010, which was the largest number of foreign-born physicians in the United States. Many of their children pursued the same profession. In August 2009, the *New York Times* carried the announcement of the marriage of Tejpreet Kaur Naakai and Karandeep Singh. Both were internal medicine doctors, and Tejpreet Nakai's father was also a physician.

The migration of technical workers from India was also impressive. Census data revealed that one-quarter of Indians were employed by companies engaged in technical and information services. When the United States began a new temporary worker program for the highly skilled in 1990, Indians received half of the visas. In California's Silicon Valley over one-third of the new companies were founded by Indian and Chinese immigrants. One person noted that when individuals in the Valley talked of "I and C" they were not "refer[ing] to integrated circuits, but to Indian and Chinese engineers."

Indians also stood out among the large numbers of foreigners enrolled in American colleges and universities in the 2000s. Computer training, science, and engineering were the main draws. Mysore Nagaraja, born in India, for example, trained in technology at the University of Utah, and was then employed by the New York City Metropolitan Transit Authority as an engineer and eventually director of the project when the city began construction of the new 2nd Avenue subway line.

Many Indians pursued the entrepreneurial route, running convenience stores such as "Seven Elevens," gas stations, and newspaper stands. Indian entrepreneurs also opened computer stores and restaurants. They were particularly involved with the hospitality industry. Kanjibhai Deswai operated the first Indian-owned motel in downtown San Francisco in the 1960s. By the end of the decade Indians owned about sixty to seventy motels in the United States. Branching out from their first individually owned establishments they then became operators of chains such as Days Inn and Holiday Inn. As early as 2000 they owned and operated one-third of America's motels. These were often labeled "potels" because so many of the owners were named Patel. The association of Indian motel management boasted eight thousand members in 2008, and a few of them sent their college-aged children to study at Cornell University's program for hotel management. In the 2000s, a small number of Indians began returning to India to set up motels and hotels in that country.

Indian immigrants in the United States came from every part of their country, but the largest number left from the western state of Gujarat. Once in America they settled where established Indian communities already existed, and in or near major university towns. Indo-American colonies could be found in the vicinity of Los Angeles, New York City, Chicago, and Houston. New Jersey's suburbs were known for their Indian populations, especially the town of Edison, near where medical facilities, drug companies, and high technical firms concentrated. In Indiana, the Asian Indian population went from 360 people in 1961 to 17,000 in 2004, a forty-fold increase. When one student in Ft. Wayne, who hailed from southern India, was asked how he would contrast people from his region with those who originated in the northern part of the country, he responded, "We eat spicy foods. They eat more like, you know, sweet foods."

Photo 5-4 There Are about 800 Hindu Temples in the United States, but None so Grand as this One in a Midwestern City

The growing Indian community, composed mostly of Sikhs and Hindus, quickly found ways to engage in religious observances. At first they met in homes and raised funds to establish appropriate temples, a few of which were quite large. In Maple Grove, Minnesota, the Indian community raised funds to build a 43,000-square-foot edifice. The price tag was nearly ten million dollars. Officially dedicated in 2008 when its tower was complete, the temple had four thousand members. The debt was high, but the Indian community had been growing, and members believed that the future was bright. These Hindus came from different parts of India and they had somewhat different customs. Remarked one leader, "It can be a challenge, but we also realize that we are so far away from home that we want to get along and work together." In any community with a significant number of Indians, summer camps were also established to instruct children in their faith.

The presence of these new institutions reflects the diversity of American religions. Exact figures for the number of Hindus in the United States are not available, as the census does not gather information about religious affiliation, but the common estimate is around one million. Indians also tried to maintain their culture by attending Indian-made "Bollywood" movies in the Hindi language. In 2007 one website posted notices of one hundred cinemas showing Bollywood films in twenty states. A patron at one observed, "What unites the people in the audience here is love of Bollywood films, and homesickness. For three hours, they are momentarily satiated by watching these creatures of light."

OTHER ASIANS

Despite the worldwide economic crisis in 2008–2009, the United States still provided incentives for prospective newcomers. Between 1990 and 2010, 130,000 Pakistanis arrived; the highest annual number was 21,555 in 2009. As their welcome in Great Britain wore thin, Pakistanis headed for the United States. Among the first arrivals were members of an educated elite, including Pakistani physicians. The Pakistani organization for doctors reported twelve thousand members in 2010. Bangladeshi immigrants in the United States have also increased numbers since the early 1990s, and many of them benefited from the diversity visas. Myanmar (formerly Burma) has sent few immigrants to the United States, mostly refugees. In 2007 thirteen thousand of them were given asylum or refugee status, and the figure increased to eighteen thousand the following year. The first Vietnamese refugees who arrived in the United States in the 1970s were only at the forefront of what later turned into a migration chain. Was it possible for the Myanmar refugees to be a similar vanguard?

POLES

At first glance it seems that Eastern Europeans should have benefited from the Hart-Celler Act of 1965. Poland and Russia together had only ten thousand places under the national origins system. However, the communist governments generally remained unwilling to see their citizens go to the United States or Western Europe. Poland, for example, had rejected many requests from citizens wishing to emigrate. After the Cold War ended in 1989 it was probably the most likely of the former communist states to allow persons to leave.

Before 1990 Poles were fleeing communism, joining relatives abroad, and seeking a better life. But the end of communism opened new doors, and in the 1990s 172,249 Poles arrived in the United States seeking economic opportunities. The potential problems in America that others warned of struck these newcomers as minor annoyances. A few thousand Polish Jews left because of anti-Semitism. They believed that the government wanted to make the nation "Judenrein [free of Jews]." One architect acknowledged, "I felt I had no future in Poland. I could be a Pole but not a Jew."

With pay so much greater in the United States than in communist Poland, many willingly risked illegal status; they did not fear being caught by immigration authorities. After 1990, the economic attraction dominated. One immigrant reported that in America the $40 pay he earned for one day's work bought enough zlotys to live in Poland for a month. Another immigrant ignored tales that asbestos removal was dangerous to one's health; he said $45 an hour trumped any other factor. Even if dangerous, he concluded, "How much more dangerous could it be than breathing the air around Katowice?"

Those with green cards settled in major cities, such as Chicago, where so many of their forbears had gone. But the center of the new Poles' lives was in the Greenpoint district of Brooklyn, New York. There Polish shops and restaurants thrived, and bakeries churned out loaves of fresh bread, which they placed in wicker baskets, just as they did when living in Poland.

However, with Poland's entry into the European Union's Common Market in 2004, the chance to build a better life was closer to home; hence many Poles went to England or Ireland to work. Moreover, the Polish economy improved substantially after the 1990s, which created employment opportunities at home. Indeed, some of America's Poles decided to return home. LOT Polish Airlines reported in 2008 that it was carrying more Poles back to Poland than the number coming to the United States, and travel agencies were selling more tickets from the United States to Poland than from Poland to the United States. Lacking readers, Marek Tomaszewski, editor of the US-based Polish-language newspaper *Polski Dzien*, said he was forced to stop publishing the newspaper in 2008. Poles who had gone to Ireland to work hurried home in 2009, when the Irish economy crashed. In 2009, Poland even found itself on the receiving end when thousands of migrants from poorer European Union nations sought work in that country.

FORMER SOVIET UNION

With the end of the Cold War Jews from the former Soviet Union were free to move, and many looked to America for a new life. They were the largest European group to immigrate to America after 1990, and their migration continued in the first decade of the twenty-first century. Over one half million arrived in that twenty-year period. At the same time, the Israeli government courted Russian Jews and many went there instead of the United States after 1990.

In 1989, New Jersey Senator Frank Lautenberg successfully sponsored an amendment to a bill in Congress to admit three hundred thousand Russian Jews, Pentecostal Christians, and Armenians. His proposal stated that the long history of Russian anti-Semitism should automatically give Jews refugee status because they were persecuted for their religious beliefs. Permitting them to enter as refugees made them eligible for special benefits.

Soviet Jews were by no means a monolithic group. Many were highly educated professionals, but some were older without skills and lacked the means to support themselves. Immigrants are normally young, but among refugee populations, such as the Russians, older members of the families traveled with their children and grandchildren. Some of the senior immigrants also suffered from poor health; hence the governments in the countries where they settled had to assume additional burdens to help these people survive.

For professionals with computer science training, opportunities abounded, and they put their training to good use after arriving in America. About fifty thousand Russian Jews settled in the Boston area and found jobs quickly. One study indicated that Boston's Soviet Jews were mainly from the urban areas; 63 percent had college degrees and 40 percent held postgraduate degrees. Although the newcomers also found well-paying jobs and received assistance in the other cities where they settled—including Baltimore, Detroit, Chicago, New York, and Los Angeles—they still had to cope with the culture shock so familiar to nearly all other immigrants and refugees.

Jews from the Russian province of Georgia usually had not experienced intense anti-Semitism and were able to practice their faith, but so many other Jews had had no religious training or knowledge of their heritage. American Jewish organizations expended much effort to acculturate them to the ways Jews lived in the United States. Some Russian Jews, however, were secular and not interested in Jewish religious and cultural organizations. In the early days of settlement in New York City, the nation's largest community of the newcomers, numbering over 200,000 in 2012, only five synagogues attracted them. Those pulled toward the synagogues were almost all people over sixty.

The first center of Soviet Jewish life in New York City was in the Brighton Beach section of Brooklyn. It had been the home of some earlier waves of Jewish immigrants. There the newcomers found a welcome, though conflicts sometimes existed between the Soviets and the more established American Jews. The long-term residents insisted that the new immigrants mainly wanted the material goods of America. One immigrant said, "It was very difficult to be a Jew in Russia. But it is not easy to be a Russian Jew in America." Soon Brighton Beach was known as "Little Odessa" because of its many Russian shops, clubs, and restaurants. The Russian language was commonly heard on the streets. While Brighton Beach was the center of the new immigrants, after first settlement many of them moved to other cities.

BOSNIANS

With the end of communism in Yugoslavia and the break-up of that nation, hostilities erupted in Bosnia among Serbs, Croatians, and Muslims. Bosnia had declared its independence from Yugoslavia in 1992. The leader of the Serbs, Slobodan Milosevic, then tried to unite the new states and used force to defeat the non-Serbs in a bloody war. After three years, a peace was finally brokered by the United States and the United Nations. By then over one million Bosnians were homeless in their own country and tens of thousands had been killed.

After the end of hostilities the United States, Germany, and Sweden, admitted many Bosnian Muslim refugees. In the United States they found homes, among other places, in Salt Lake City, Chicago, and St. Louis. Eventually over one hundred thousand were brought to the United States, where networks of earlier immigrants helped them to acculturate. The refugees in turn began to sponsor their relatives. Their settlement in the United States has been difficult in spite of the economic assistance they were entitled to as refugees. Many Bosnians had witnessed the horrors of violence and the annihilation of families. Moreover, the Bosnian Muslims, who formed the majority of the refugees, were entering a predominately Christian society at a time when Islam was equated with terrorism in the minds of many Americans, an effect of terrorists' destruction of New York City's World

Photo 5-5 Travel Agency Specializing in Trips Home to Poland with the National Airline of Poland (LOT)

Trade Center in 2001. One observer noted that they were "the right color" but "the wrong religion."

Nevertheless, Bosnians have managed to create new lives in America. The center of Bosnian life in the United States was St. Louis, which had an estimated fifty thousand of these refugees. There they operated small businesses and formed organizations to aid the community. In 2009 they opened a Bosnian Chamber of Commerce, the first in the United States. The facility was formerly a theater and was renovated with federal aid and local funding. Bosnians in St. Louis even published a newspaper, *Sabah*.

Overall European immigration grew after the Cold War ended. The Berlin Wall fell in November 1989, and in the next decade 1.3 million European immigrants, nearly double the number of the 1980s, arrived in America. After 2000 the exodus from former communist nations in Eastern Europe dropped, and European immigration to the United States slowed. For example, Poles averaged seventeen thousand annually in the 1990s but only half that figure in the 2000s.

Despite the hundreds of thousands of Europeans added to the American population, there was a major shift in the patterns of immigration after 1965. Whereas in 1965 about 80 percent of immigrants hailed from Europe, by 2010 Europeans represented only 15 percent of the new arrivals. By the end of the first decade of the twenty-first century, the vast majority of newcomers came from Latin

America, Asia, the Middle East, Africa, and the Caribbean. Latinos were especially prominent, constituting the largest group of immigrants in the last half century. The new immigrants have settled in every part of the country, and communities that once thought of themselves as one homogeneous group suddenly discovered different cultural groups settling in their midst. As with new immigrants in the past, American communities generally found fault with people of different back-grounds who spoke little or no English, who worshiped in unaccustomed ways, and who were often resistant to social intercourse with long-standing residents in the area. To be sure, new ethnics "upset the apple cart," and both old and new resi-dents needed to accommodate one another. Sometimes the adjustments took years, other times it took decades. However, Americans and their immigrants ultimately blended together, and today it is difficult, if not impossible, to differentiate people whose ancestors came in the colonial era from those whose forbears arrived only forty or fifty years ago. Second- and third-generation Americans often behave in the same fashion, and have the same values, as those who are sixth-, seventh-, and eighth-generation citizens. This amalgamation of cultures is one of the outstand-ing characteristics of Americans. And, despite the influences of various foreign ways and values, American culture has always trumped that of every other group of immigrants over the past four centuries.

CHAPTER 6

American Immigration
and the Interconnected World

The post-1945 immigrants had a major impact on American society, just as the generations who came before them did; the influence was especially noticeable after 1970. As was discussed earlier, the number of Latinos, Asians, Middle Easterners, and Africans rose dramatically. The signs of immigration were everywhere. During a period when newspapers generally were struggling due to declining readerships, more foreign-language newspapers appeared on newsstands. The number of television programs grew as well, with Spanish programs being the most numerous and popular. The largest Spanish-language television network, Univision, competed in its audience share with the major national stations; in 2010, it ranked fifth among all telecasters. Drama and music created and performed by the latest newcomers became common, especially after 1990, with so many immigrants dispersed throughout the United States. Hospitals, police departments, and judicial courts scrambled for persons who could speak foreign languages to serve as translators. Moreover, most large—and some small—cities and suburbs boasted a great variety of ethnic restaurants.

Perhaps the two most important areas of immigrant influence were religion and the economy. In 2010, the United States was among the most religious nations in the world, with a large percent of the population belonging to a church and attending worship services. Fewer than 20 percent of Americans were nonbelievers, although their numbers had been growing in recent years. Hispanics comprised nearly 40 percent of the members of the Roman Catholic Church and a higher proportion of those under the age of twenty-one. Haitian, Filipino, and Vietnamese immigrants also augmented the Catholic Church's rolls, which otherwise would have faced a decline. In 2010 two social scientists, Robert D. Putnam and David E. Campbell, put it bluntly, "Except for the timely arrival of large numbers of Latino immigrants, the future of the American Catholic Church might appear bleak." To meet the challenges of serving new immigrants, the Catholic Church had to scramble for Spanish-speaking priests and nuns, and not with great success.

Among the nation's Protestants, membership in the more established denominations had been static or even decreasing for several decades. However, Korean Protestants filled the empty churches for their growing congregations in order to hold services in their native language. The number of Pentecostal Hispanics also increased, with many of their services conducted in store-front churches. The exact numbers were unknown, but these congregations were numerous enough for Catholic leaders to become alarmed. The number of Chinese Protestant churches also grew during the past forty years, but their numbers were not significant.

The most striking religious development after 1970 was the immigration of non-Christians. The number of Asian Indian Sikhs and Hindus rose rapidly to support an estimated eight hundred temples. While this number was not especially large in 2010, it reflected a relatively new diversity of religion in the United States. Sikhs were smaller in number, as were Buddhists. Sacramento, California, for example, a city that has seen a large rise in its immigration population in the last two decades, has 58 churches, mostly in the city's surrounding areas. They include Buddhist, Hindu, Sikh, and Tao temples, mosques, Vietnamese Catholic churches, and Protestant Iglesias.

The major non-Christian immigrant group after 1945 was Muslim, and the role of Islam in American society caused more anxiety among non-Muslim Americans. The exact number of Muslims in the United States in 2010 was not known; some

Photo 6-1 No Immigrant Group Has Been so Important for American Protestantism than Koreans

estimates ran as high as seven million, but others placed their number at 1.5 million. However, one thing was clear: the American Muslim community was more diverse than any other Islamic community in the world. As many as 40 percent were African Americans—not immigrants—with roughly 30 percent coming from the Middle East and another 30 percent from Asia and Africa. Followers of Islam thus represented a great variety of nationalities, religious practices, and languages.

As noted, following the terrorist attacks of September 11, 2001 (9/11) when New York City's World Trade Center was destroyed, Congress passed several laws aimed at keeping out terrorists, deported hundreds of Arabs and Muslims, and set up surveillance on several mosques thought to be headed by radical imams (the title held by Muslim worship leaders). Subsequent events added to the hostility toward Islam, as several Muslims with Middle Eastern family origins were arrested and convicted of plotting to detonate bombs, and of ties to Al Qaeda, the terrorist group responsible for the events of 9/11. A failed attempt to set off a car bomb in 2010 in New York City's Time Square led to the arrest and conviction of a radical Pakistani-born US citizen, Faisal Shahzad.

Perhaps the most chilling incident occurred at Fort Hood, Texas, in November 2009, when an American-born army psychiatrist, whose parents had emigrated from Jordan, shot and killed thirteen people and wounded many more. According to the investigation that followed, he was opposed to the US wars in Iraq and Afghanistan and had been in contact with an extremist imam in Yemen. Such events were highly unusual. Actually investigators found little connection between Muslims and terrorism or violence in the years following 9/11. A study by a North Carolina research group revealed that in 2011 of the 14,000 murders in the United States in 2011 not a single one was resulted from Islamic terrorism. The author of the report called Muslim Americans "a minuscule threat to public safety."

A heated controversy arose in 2010 when New York City issued a permit to build an Islamic community center two blocks from the where the World Trade Center had once stood. Almost immediately protests arose; opponents of the permit claimed that it was an insult to have the center so close to the site known as "ground zero." Michael Bloomberg, the city's mayor, defended the proposal, as did the city commission that had approved building the center. Yet polls indicated that a majority of New Yorkers opposed the plan as did a number of politicians and organizations. Abdul Rauf, the imam in charge of the project, was known to be a man who reached out to various ethnic and religious groups; he had even been sent by the United States State Department to Egypt on a goodwill mission. While the center would house a mosque, it was also designed as a place to bring religious groups together and provide services to the surrounding community. Despite public outcry, city officials stood firm about permitting the center to go forward. However, funding to build the center remained a problem even after a new Islamic group took over the project.

Manhattan was not the only place where controversies over mosques and Muslim community centers occurred. In New York City's borough of Staten Island, opposition to the building of a mosque led to the cancellation of the project. In Sheboygan, Wisconsin, local ministers led protests against a proposed mosque; a similar incident occurred in Murfreesboro, Tennessee. North of San Diego, angry opponents confronted a proposal to construct an Islamic center. One woman insisted that Islam was not a religion and declared that in "20 years with the rate of birth [of the Muslim] population, we will be overtaken by Islam, and their goal is to get people in Congress and the Supreme Court to see that Shariah [Islamic law] is implanted. My children and grandchildren will have to live under that." It should be emphasized, however, that of the estimated nineteen hundred mosques in the United States, the overwhelming majority encountered no problems.

The hijab or head scarf, is not obligatory for Muslim women; some women reject it entirely while others choose to wear it as a sign of their faith. Some non-Muslim Americans believed that women who wore the hijab were potential terrorists, possibly because these non-Muslims wrongly equated Muslim religious observance with anti-American beliefs. Hence, wearing the hijab caused problems for some Muslim women. Dozens of Muslim women reported being denied employment by companies including Domino's Pizza, Sears, J.C. Penney, and Office Depot. As a result, some companies changed their policies to allow Muslim women to wear the hijab at work.

AN IMMIGRANT'S TALE

In 2010 an American Muslim flight attendant at U.S. Airlines who had worked for the company for more than ten years was fired for wearing a scarf, called a hijab in her religious faith, to work. Although the woman behaved like other American women in her daily customs—she drove an American-made car, shopped at the mall, and headed a local Girl Scout troop, U.S. Air objected to her observing an aspect of her faith during working hours. The fired flight attendant brought a complaint to the EEOC (Equal Employment Opportunity Commission) for religious discrimination, a violation of the United States Civil Rights Act of 1964.

After hearing the case the EEOC and U.S. Airways settled with a compromise.

The airline would reemploy the young woman but only as a cleaning person on the airlines; it would not rehire her as a flight attendant. The former flight attendant was not pleased. She noted, "in this day and age, everyone is looking for diversity in the workplace, and diversity sensitivity, and yet when you have the diversity, you're stifling it."

This discrimination in the workplace was not an isolated event. The Council on American Islamic Relations reported in 2010 that complaints of discrimination against Muslim women more than doubled between 2001 and 2009.

A growing number of other Muslims also reported job discrimination in the late 2000s, including harassment and taunts in the workplace. Some asserted that they had been called "terrorists" or "Osama," the first name of Al Qaeda's leader at the time of the 9/11 terrorist attacks. The Equal Employment Opportunity Commission (EEOC) confirmed a sharp increase in the number of complaints. In 2009, although Muslims represented less than 2 percent of the total population, they constituted one-quarter of complaints based on religion. One federal official with the EEOC in Phoenix, Arizona, said, "I've been doing this for 32 years, and I've never seen such antipathy toward Muslim workers."

The impact by the new immigrants on the American economy was also important, but like religion it sometimes caused conflict. Immigrants came to the United States to work or to be with family, but some anti-immigration pundits argued that they lived off of welfare. While the foreign-born population was just under 13 percent of the total US population in 2010, immigrants comprised 15 percent of the workforce, and the numbers of working immigrants actually increased during the recession that began in 2008.

Accusations that the newcomers relied on American welfare benefits prompted the federal government in the mid-1990s to exclude immigrants from certain welfare programs. The issue was complicated, however, because immigrant households often contained foreign-born parents with children born in the United States who qualified for social services denied to noncitizens. The denial of benefits partially accounted for the large increase in the number of immigrants becoming US citizens in the 1990s. Over time, the federal government restored some of the cuts, while some states reinstated or added other programs.

It appeared that the pattern of employment of immigrants was shaped like an hourglass, with the highly educated and skilled immigrants at the top doing well, and the poorly educated who lacked English language skills remaining at the bottom. Twenty-eight percent of persons with doctoral degrees, for example, were immigrants, even though their percent of the population as a whole was less than half that figure. Overall, immigrants were disproportionately represented among the professional classes. One could easily point to foreign-born doctors, especially Asian Indian physicians, or computer-oriented Chinese starting their own businesses, as examples.

At the bottom of the occupational hierarchy were those immigrants with no high school diploma and poor English who labored in construction and landscaping or stood on street corners waiting to be picked up for a day of labor. They also cleaned rooms in hotels, bused tables and washed dishes in restaurants, did housework, or worked in immigrant niches such as nail salons. Many of these workers were from Mexico and Central America. Thirty-six percent of all immigrants lacked a high school diploma, compared with almost 10 percent of native-born Americans. Because immigrants made up a relatively high percentage of those in low-wage jobs, some claimed that newcomers depressed the wages of uneducated Americans. However, there was slight evidence for this contention. Studies also showed that many immigrants were located in the middle level of the employment

Photo 6-2 President Barrack Obama at the Swearing in of New Citizens

structure. Some were entrepreneurs who ran small businesses; others worked in health care, and still others in white-collar positions in the fast-growing service industries. Frequently, immigrants who owned small businesses employed both members of their own ethnic group and others.

Political discussions about the foreign-born raised other issues, especially concerning undocumented immigrants and the large numbers of Hispanic new-comers. A few members of Congress wrote books or proposed legislation calling for decreases in immigration, and many people claimed that Hispanics, and especially Mexicans, were undermining the nation's Anglo-Saxon cultural heritage. There was little evidence to show that Mexicans were different from earlier immigrants who became part of the American mainstream within a generation or two. Because of the large scale of Hispanic immigrants who lacked English, it appeared that many were not becoming Americanized, but their children and grandchildren spoke English, acquired more education than their parents, and had better jobs. Moreover, many Hispanics were marrying non-Hispanic whites. Today it is almost impossible to find Germans or English who married only members of their nationality. Those who opposed immigration often focused their wrath on undocumented immigrants. Former television pundit Lou Dobbs frequently assailed these newcomers and urged the deportation of those without legal documents, while organizations such as the Federation for American Immigration Reform, the Center for Immigration Studies, and NumbersUSA led the attack to reduce existing levels of immigration.

AN IMMIGRANT'S TALE

On November 8, 2008, Marcelo Lucero, an Ecuadorian immigrant, was murdered in the town of Patchogue, New York. The police said the killing was carried out by a gang of youths called the Caucasian Crew. Some officials said this was an isolated incident, but ethnic hatred was not unusual in that community, and some of the bigotry led to ethnic violence. The Southern Poverty Law Center (SPLC), an Atlanta organization that follows ethnic and racial violence, decided to investigate. In a report issued in August, 2009, a Spanish-speaking investigator found that the town had experienced a number of hate crimes directed against Latinos in recent years. The SPLC pointed out that politicians had actually encouraged violence. One county legislator had previously said that if he saw an influx of Hispanics in his town, "we'll be out with baseball bats." Another warned that undocumented immigrants had "better be aware."

In another investigation, several Latinos gave their accounts of living in Suffolk County on Long Island, New York. What emerged from their statements was a fear of living in the area. One man from Peru said he feared walking in the streets, while another said he had rocks thrown at him. Still another claimed hostile residents shot at him and they stole his bike. If they were the victims of such crimes they nonetheless reported that they believed the police would do nothing to those guilty of violence, or for that matter, even stealing their bikes. These young immigrants provided stories that could be repeated in other communities as well.

Opponents of immigration were unable to change policies to reduce legal immigration; however, their focus on curtailing undocumented immigration was more successful. There were two ways the federal government could control illegal immigration: First, by blocking the employment of such migrants and second, by improving enforcement of border controls. When Congress passed the Immigration Reform and Control Act of 1986 (IRCA), legislators struck a bargain to win an amnesty for millions of undocumented aliens, people who had entered the United States before 1982, or those who had engaged in agricultural work for a few months between 1984 and 1985. In exchange for these amnesties, Congress outlawed the employment of undocumented immigration. The law called for penalties on employers who hired undocumented immigrants knowingly, but federal agents rarely enforced this provision. There was no easy way to prove that employers knew if the documents their employees had shown them in order to obtain work were fraudulent; thus employers could maintain that so long as they had examined the documents, they met the law's requirement. Moreover, Congress did not appropriate funds for an adequate number of inspectors.

However, in 2005, the Bush administration decided to enforce employer sanctions by stepping up the pace of inspection. More businesses suspected of hiring undocumented workers were raided and unauthorized workers deported. President Barack Obama promised to focus more attention on employers who violated the law and less on employees. His administration expended greater resources to arrest and prosecute those who smuggled immigrants into the United States. The Obama administration also said that in view of limited resources the government would concentrate on deporting those who had been convicted of serious offenses. Both the Bush and Obama administrations stepped up the deportation of immigrants, legal and illegal. The number of those deported from the United States reached nearly four hundred thousand in 2009. Some politicians suggested that undocumented immigrants who had been brought to the United States as children should not be deported if they continued their educations or served in the military. This suggestion was put forth as the "Dream Act," but Republicans in Congress refused to pass it. The act could cover over 1 million undocumented immigrants. President Obama in 2012 ordered that such persons should not be deported, but his order covered only a two year period. It remained uncertain whether Congress would pass the "Dream Act" and grant these immigrants legal status.

The second way in which the government could deal with undocumented immigration was to seal the border. Over the years Congress increased the number of agents in the Border Patrol. In 2006, the Republican-dominated House of Representatives passed a law supporting the building of additional walls along the US-Mexico border as well as making it a crime to assist unauthorized immigrants in any way. Latinos were angry about Republican support for the new wall. Hispanic leaders supported legalization of undocumented immigrants and large increases in temporary worker programs, but their views had little influence on members of Congress. However, they did rally Hispanic votes for the Democrats in national elections.

A Senate committee, led by Senators John McCain and Edward Kennedy, took up its own immigration bill in 2006 and again in 2007. The Senate version included a temporary worker program for four hundred thousand low-wage workers. This proposal angered those who believed that such legislation provided only slight protection for temporary immigrant laborers; they pointed to the Bracero Program and studies of other smaller programs that had offered little protection for immigrant workers. Another provision in the Senate bill for an eventual legalization process for undocumented workers also drew opposition; opponents complained that such a system would be nothing more than another amnesty, and they argued that the amnesty passed in 1986 had failed to halt future undocumented immigration. Ultimately, the proposal never saw the light of day, and the Senate never had a chance to vote on it.

All that remained from the attempts in both the House and Senate to deal with unauthorized immigration along the border with Mexico was appropriation for seven hundred miles of new fencing; a "virtual" fence elsewhere (with lights

Photo 6-3 Undocumented Immigrants in Detention Waiting Deportation

and equipment); and a large increase in the Border Patrol. The fence was slow to be built, but by 2010 it was nearly finished. Then it ran into funding problems, as did the new technology being instituted along the border between the United States and Mexico; both proved too costly to finance during the economic downturn at that time. Although completion of the fence was forestalled, the Border Patrol boasted twenty thousand employees in 2010, up from three thousand in 1986, when Congress enacted IRCA. Proponents of stronger measures could take heart from public opinion polls that generally supported a tough stance on border controls and support for a decrease in all immigration. However, the mounting costs of enforcement during a major recession made many members of Congress reluctant to spend more.

In 2012 the Department of Homeland Security reported that the number of legal immigrants was about the same from 2009 to 2011, running about one million each year. The backlog of persons awaiting visas to the United States was over three million. Thus, if some were eligible but decided against entry into the United States, others were willing to come in their stead. Legal immigrants, as was noted earlier, came for a variety of reasons, including work, family reunification, and political asylum, or as refugees. Undocumented immigrants, on the other hand, came mainly to find employment.

The US federal government estimated that the undocumented population had increased substantially in the early 2000s, before a decline from 11.8 million in 2008 to 10.8 million in 2009. Then it stayed about the same in 2010 and 2011 at approximately 11.5 million. There was also a large drop in the number of persons trying to cross into the United States. Supporters of tougher enforcement contended that the huge increase in the Border Patrol and more worksite inspections were responsible for the drop in the number of apprehensions of undocumented persons. They pointed to the fact that for Mexicans alone the drop was huge. In 2005 the Border Patrol apprehended more than one million Mexicans trying to cross into the United States illegally, but in 2011 the figure was only 286,000. Overall, in early 2009 Mexico reported a huge decline in the number of its nationals emigrating to the United States. It should be noted that in late 2007 jobs in construction fell, and the US and the global economy entered the worst recession since the Great Depression of the 1930s, severely limiting economic opportunities, particularly for low-wage workers. Moreover, in recent years the Mexican birthrate had dropped, thus easing pressure for finding new jobs, and the Mexican economy had improved. By 2011 the number of Mexicans in the United States had not increased. The number arriving was roughly the same as those heading back home.

Because Congress failed to reach an accord that prevented illegal immigration, frustrated state and local governments took up the challenge. Texas and California passed laws to deal with the rising numbers of immigrants in their states by requiring local officials to ascertain the legal status of anyone arrested on other charges. They were not alone: literally hundreds of measures addressing immigration were debated at the state level. In 2007, fourteen hundred immigration-related bills were introduced in state legislatures throughout the country, though only a few actually became law. In 2009 Arizona passed a statute allowing police officers to request documents of persons to prove that they were in the United States legally. This law resulted in vocal outcries of both support and outrage throughout the country. In 2012 the US Supreme Court upheld only one provision of the Arizona law, but it was the most important one: the police had the right to ask for proof of citizenship or legal status from people who were stopped for suspected violations of the law. However, the decision left many provisions of other such laws open to future court contests. While in many places local authorities cooperated with the federal government in deporting undocumented immigrants, in other areas local officials refused to turn over persons who had been arrested on minor charges and found to be in the country illegally. When a court upheld a particularly harsh Alabama law in 2011, thousands of Alabama Hispanic immigrants fled their communities.

One of the salient issues for states was education: should undocumented children be allowed to attend schools? The US Supreme Court ruled in 1982 that undocumented children could not be barred from attending public schools; nor could states refuse to reimburse local school districts' per-pupil funding for students who were illegal immigrants. However, many communities faced the need to build new schools for their burgeoning immigrant populations, with little recourse to state or federal funds. School districts also needed to hire more educators, particularly bilingual ones, to teach the newcomers. To avoid the expense of hiring bilingual teachers, some local communities looked to state governments to ban bilingual education. A few states responded; in California, voters passed a referendum prohibiting bilingual education programs in the public schools. In a related issue, states struggled with whether undocumented students should pay the same tuition as state residents in institutions of higher education, or if they even had the right to attend state colleges and universities. Some states, including New York and Utah, allowed undocumented persons to pay in-state tuition rates; other states prohibited undocumented persons from enrolling in public colleges and universities.

Another state issue involved issuing drivers' licenses to unauthorized immigrants. Some proponents of undocumented aliens to obtain drivers' licenses argued that many were already driving; it was preferable to test them than to have them drive without a license or auto insurance. In 2008 New York Governor Eliot Spitzer supported such a proposal, but the legislature failed to enact it. A more critical—and costly—state concern was the provision of health care. Immigrants, especially undocumented ones, often lacked health insurance. Should state-supported hospitals and medical clinics be required to accept them as patients as was the case for other low-income residents? California had been admitting undocumented immigrants to hospitals, but as a result of the recession, the state indicated in 2009 that it would provide health care to illegal immigrants only in emergencies. States also grappled with the issue of workmen's compensation insurance, which was a major concern, considering the physical risks involved in construction and other low-skilled labor. In 2006, a New York state court held that undocumented immigrants were entitled to payment for injuries on the job. Three years later, three undocumented immigrants were awarded a total of $3.85 million for their employment-related injuries.

Although setting and enforcing immigration policy was ultimately the responsibility of the federal government, the costs fell disproportionately on those communities and states that saw the most significant increases in the number of newcomers. In addition to education and health care, states also extended welfare benefits and fire and police protection with little reimbursement from the federal government. True, working immigrants—including many illegal ones—paid taxes, but the major recipient of this revenue was the federal government, primarily through Social Security and Medicare taxes. State and local governments had to scramble to finance programs for their new residents.

Beyond the debates about immigration were important issues for the nation to resolve. Certainly the development of a multicultural American society provided great benefits to all its residents in an increasingly interconnected world. The United States lacked Arabic speakers and expertise when it decided to intervene militarily in the Middle East. In addition, it was an advantage to have persons knowledgeable about other societies' cultures and economies when Americans conducted business outside the United States.

The United States was by no means the only nation to be affected by large-scale immigration after 1945. Australia changed its whites-only immigration policy and by the 1970s was admitting Asians as well as Europeans. To be sure, Australia struggled with the questions of how many persons to admit and who should receive asylum. In the 2000s, boats appeared off the Australian coast with passengers from Sri Lanka seeking asylum. The government decided to hold the petitioners on Christmas Island off the coast while the cases were being decided. Like many nations in recent years, Australia feared that a lax asylum policy would only encourage other asylum-seekers.

Canada too changed its laws after World War II and had perhaps the most liberal policy of receiving nations. No longer did Canada accept only Europeans; the newcomers after 1948 came from Asia, the Caribbean, and Africa as well as Europe. Nor did Canada witness the development of groups or political parties dedicated to keeping rates of immigration low. Canada, of course, did not have a southern neighbor such as Mexico with people clamoring for employment abroad. Canada also had a large land mass that was sparsely populated. Yet overall, the foreign-born population of Canada constituted 20 percent of the nation's population in 2010, whereas in the United States the figure was 12.6 percent. Canada also adopted "multiculturalism" as an official policy.

While Canada accepted multiculturalism and the United States called itself a "nation of immigrants," in Europe the situation was more complex. Western European nations had been receiving immigrants before 1945, but they were mostly from Southern and Eastern Europe and numbers were small. Europe during the period from 1800 through the 1920s was experiencing greater emigration than immigration, mainly to the United States, Canada, Australia, and South America. Other Europeans headed toward newly colonized regions in Asia and Africa as agents of colonialism.

After World War II, the first major immigration crisis occurred in Germany. As noted earlier, nations of Central and Eastern Europe deported eleven million persons of German heritage who were believed to have been Nazi sympathizers during the war. Germany absorbed these exiled persons rather quickly, and by the late 1950s, the German economy was experiencing labor shortages. To resolve this problem, the German government recruited temporary workers, usually males for low-skilled jobs, from countries like Italy, Portugal, Spain, Greece, and especially Turkey. The recession of 1973 brought a halt to this program. Germans planned for these workers to be temporary migrants, and many Italians, for example, returned home when Italy's economy improved. However, many of the Turks remained and brought their families to join them. Germany was reluctant to deport them because memories of the Holocaust made its government particularly sensitive about treatment of minorities in its midst. As a result, German society now included a mostly lower-class group of Muslim Middle Eastern immigrants and their descendents.

Some other nations in Western Europe also received numerous migrants. France accepted a large number of Portuguese in the 1950s and 1960s and later Muslims from North Africa. In the early days of the Cold War, Great Britain gave refuge and granted asylum to Poles who refused to return to communist Poland. Other refugees from the Cold War followed; Czech protesters from the failed uprising against their communist government in 1968 also found a home in Great Britain. Yet for the most part, Europeans did not perceive their nations as immigrant destinations. A 1977 report of the German government, for example,

Table 6.1 Foreign-Born Population in Selected European Nations (2005)

NATION	FOREIGN-BORN PERCENT OF THE TOTAL
Austria	15.1
Denmark	7.2
France	10.7
Germany	12.3
Italy	4.5
Netherlands	10.1
Portugal	7.3
Sweden	12.4
United Kingdom (Great Britain)	9.1

SOURCE: Organization for Economic Co-operation and Development, *UN Migration Database*, 2010.

declared, "Germany is not an immigrant country." However, as the table above demonstrates, many European countries had sizable numbers of immigrants.

As discussed earlier, the second large-scale immigration to Europe took place when colonies in Asia and Africa achieved independence. With self-governance in place in these new nations, the European former officials returned to their native lands. Some had lived for several generations in Africa or Asia, but they nonetheless saw their futures as limited, and most still identified as Europeans. They were quickly followed by many of the formerly colonized people. Some European nations had considered their overseas subjects to be full citizens with the right of immigration during the colonial period. However, when the numbers of black West Indians and South Asian immigrants grew in Great Britain, and the numbers of Algerians increased in France, these governments began to place restrictions on immigration from their former colonies.

In the 1990s the almost constant violence in the Middle East drove a new stream of immigrants from their homes: Lebanese, Afghans, and Iranians, to Europe and the United States. The violence in the Balkans also disrupted nations, and many Bosnians fled to Germany or the United States. Moreover, persons who had been unable to leave the Soviet Union, Poland, or other communist nations flocked to the west after 1990, especially Germany, when their communist governments collapsed and the new regimes lifted bans on emigration. Moreover, military conflicts, famines, and poverty in Africa stimulated others to look to Europe as the place to improve their lives. When Europe began limiting immigration through regular channels, applying as a refugee or seeking asylum became more common, because European nations were sympathetic to people escaping from dangerous situations. However, if foreigners could not enter legally, many tried to come and remain without legal papers, just as they did in Australia, Canada, or the United States. The asylum-seekers rose sharply in 2011, when Arab nations in northern Africa erupted into violence, forcing many persons to flee to southern Europe.

Nations such as Italy were not happy to see these newcomers and other members of the European Union were faced with a difficult situation. It was not clear how Europe would ultimately deal with the latest influx.

Germany had the most generous policies in Europe to aid the newcomers, though most were only granted temporary status rather than asylum. Germany received 438,191 petitions for asylum in 1992 and 322,599 the next year, by far the largest number in the European Union. However, the cost of assimilating a much poorer eastern Germany was too high for many West Germans, and the unsettled conditions in the east, along with relatively high unemployment, led to the rise of neo-Nazi groups protesting more foreigners. From 1990 to 1992, Germany witnessed a series of violent attacks on non-Germans, and the hate groups called for the halt of the generous asylum system. Hate crimes diminished when the number of asylum-seekers fell after 2000 and as the former East Germany began to experience an improved economy.

Another factor complicating immigration in Europe was the attempt through the European Union to have uniform policies across Europe, even though different countries had different populations. This issue was compounded by the fact that citizens of the European Community had the right to migrate to any other member nation. However, such movements did not always lead to employment, nor were foreigners always warmly received.

The presence of so many newcomers triggered opposition to immigrants in nations other than Germany. In Austria, politician Jorg Haider led the Freedom Party that reviled foreigners. In 1999, his party's popularity peaked with 27 percent of the voters, but as prosperity returned, his party fell out of favor, receiving only 6.4 percent of the vote in 2004. In France, the Front National, led by Jean-Marie Le Pen, took up the cause of right-wing politics in 1990s and directed its anti-immigrant rhetoric primarily against North Africans. Many citizens of Great Britain and Denmark also claimed that the "boat was full," and that large numbers of foreigners were not welcome.

Much of the opposition to foreigners was no doubt based on racism and nationalism, but nativist sentiment was also roused by the fact that many of the newcomers were Muslims. In 2010 France had the largest Islamic population in Europe, with twenty-four hundred mosques, followed by Germany and Great Britain. These nations witnessed demonstrations and anti-immigrant violence; some then passed laws against Muslims. In France the hijab, or head scarf, that some Muslim women choose to wear, was banned in public schools; elsewhere violence erupted against immigrants and their children, raising the question of how many Muslims non-Muslim Europeans would tolerate in their midst.

Perhaps the most sensational recent case was that of Thilo Sarrazin, a high official with Germany's central bank, who caused a furor when he published a book in 2010 assailing Muslims. His publication hit a nerve and quickly sold over one million copies. It argued that the high birthrate among Muslims and their lack of integration into German society made them a threat to the nation's future. He also alleged that intelligence was inherited and that Muslims were intellectually inferior. Shocking to all Europeans was the slaughter of 77 persons by Norwegian Anders Behring Breivik in July 2011. He was connected to groups that believed that the ethnic and religious make up of Europe should not be changed.

Behind much of this anti-Muslim message, which was also heard in the United States, was the connection between demographics and immigration. The falling birthrate among non-Muslim Europeans raised concerns about who would pay for the generous welfare benefits in most European nations, especially as large numbers of workers retired. Either taxes would have to be raised or benefits substantially cut if not enough workers were found to maintain the welfare state. Clearly immigrant laborers were needed. In the beginning of the twenty-first century, Japan faced a similar problem, but the Japanese showed little enthusiasm for admitting immigrants. Many European leaders were aware of the growing shortage of workers and called for more immigration, especially in the skilled professions. In the future, this could lead to competition for highly educated newcomers.

Finally, immigration policy involved ethical issues. The United States took in over one million South Asians as a result of its involvement in the Vietnam War. What was the nation's moral obligation to the several million Iraqis displaced by the US war in Iraq, or to refugees from clashes between American troops and insurgents in Afghanistan? What of humanitarian considerations for other refugees in the world? Or asylum petitions granted to those persecuted by their own repressive governments, particularly ones allied with or supported by the United States? What did the relatively rich societies of the world owe to the less fortunate, particularly those on whom they relied for cheap labor or natural resources? Many of these countries did not offer worker or environmental protections that would make the goods and services they sold on the world market more expensive for wealthier nations. These questions continued to pose a conundrum going into the twenty-first century to people throughout the world. While it was difficult to foresee how nations would deal with immigration policy in the future, it was clear that immigration would remain a major—and contentious-issue.

As these chapters make clear, the United States has become a diverse society since the end of World War II. The immigration of so many newcomers from around the world has changed America from a nation of European-origin peoples to a multicultural one. The issue for the future is not that America will become even more diverse. Rather the issue will be the nature of that diversity, and immigration will play the key role in the new multicultural nation, at least in the immediate future.

Appendix 1
Major Laws and Actions

1942   The United States and Mexico agree to the Bracero Program, permitting temporary foreign laborers to work in the United States.

1943   Congress repeals the ban on Chinese immigration.

1945   Congress passes the War Brides Act, facilitating the entry of alien wives, husbands, and children of members of the US armed forces.

1948   Congress enacts the Displaced Persons Act, allowing the entrance of 205,000 displaced persons in addition to those admitted under the annual quotas.

1950   Congress amends the Displaced Persons Act and adds 200,000 to the numbers to be admitted under its provisions.

1952   Congress passes the McCarran-Walter Immigration and Naturalization Act, which

- eliminates race as a bar to immigration and naturalization;
- reaffirms the national origins system but gives every nation a quota;
- provides for a more thorough screening of immigrants;
- establishes preferences for those with relatives in America or those with skills.

1953   Congress enacts the Refugee Relief Act, authorizing the admission of special nonquota refugees.

1957   Congress passes the Refugee Escape Act, liberalizing the McCarran-Walter Act and allowing more nonquota immigrants to enter.

1960   Congress passes the World Refugee Year Law, permitting the entrance of additional refugees.

1962   Congress enacts the Migration and Refugee Assistance Act, facilitating the admission of refugees.

1964   The United States and Mexico terminate the Bracero Program.

1965   Congress passes the Immigration Act of 1965, which

— abolishes the national origins system;
— establishes a limit of 170,000 from outside the Western Hemisphere and a limit of 20,000 from any one country;
— admits immigrants on a first-come, first-qualified basis;
— establishes preferences for close relatives as well as refugees and those with occupational skills needed in the United States;
— places a ceiling of 120,000 on immigration from the Western Hemisphere.

1976   Congress extends the 20,000 limit per country to the Western Hemisphere and establishes a modified preference system for the hemisphere.

1978   Congress establishes a single worldwide ceiling of 290,000 for the admission of immigrants and a uniform preference system.

1978   Congress creates a Select Commission on Immigration and Refugee Policy to study and evaluate existing immigration policy.

1980   Congress passes the Refugee Act of 1980, which

— increases the total annual immigration to 320,000;
— increases the number of refugees from 17,400 to 50,000 annually;
— defines "refugee" to include people from any part of the world, not just the Middle East or communist countries;
— creates the office of US Coordinator for Refugee Affairs.

1986   Congress passes the Immigration Reform and Control Act, which

— prohibits employers from knowingly employing undocumented aliens;
— grants an amnesty to those who came illegally to the United States before 1982 and a second amnesty to some farm workers and makes it possible for them to become resident aliens and US citizens;
— provides for the admission of temporary farm workers.

1990   Congress passes the Immigration Act of 1990, which

— increases immigration (excluding refugees) to 700,000 until 1995, when it becomes 675,000. The limit can be exceeded;
— increases employment visas to 140,000 from 54,000;
— creates a new category for "diversity visas." Beginning in 1995 it provided for 55,000 visas annually. Later it was made 50,000.

1992   Congress passes the Chinese Student Protection Act, which permits Chinese students in the United States from June 1989 to April 1990 to adjust their status to become immigrants.

| 1996 | Congress passes a new welfare law that limits some federal benefits for immigrants. |
| 1996 | Congress passes the Illegal Immigration Reform and Immigrant Responsibility Act, which |

- authorizes new border fences and increases size of INS;
- tightens restrictions on illegal immigrants to make it easier to deport them;
- tightens procedures for asylum-seekers;
- institutes pilot programs for verification of immigration status for those seeking employment;
- makes sponsors of new immigrants more responsible for their welfare.

1997	Congress passes the Nicaraguan Adjustment and Central American Relief Act, which grants an amnesty to some Central Americans.
2001	Congress passes the USA Patriot Act, which tightens rules for entrance to the United States, especially for males from the Middle East.
2003	Reorganization of the Immigration and Naturalization Service (and other agencies) into the Department of Homeland Security. Border enforcement now under Immigration and Customs Enforcement (ICE).
2006	National Guard sent to US-Mexican border to aid the Border Patrol in halting influx of undocumented aliens trying to cross the border.
2007	Increased enforcement of the Employers' Sanctions.
2007–2011	Increased funding for ICE and border agents. Number of agents increased to 20,000 by 2011.
2007–2011	Building of 700-mile wall and other barriers along the US-Mexican border. Construction halted in 2011 due to costs.
2010	Deportation of immigrants approaches 400,000.

SOURCES

Edward P. Hutchinson, *Legislative History of American Immigration Policy, 1798–1965* (Philadelphia: University of Pennsylvania Press, 1981); US Congress, Senate Committee on the Judiciary, *U.S. Immigration Law and Policy; 1952–1979*; The Congressional Research Service, 96th Congress, 1st session, *Congressional Quarterly* (1980, 1986); *Statistical Yearbook* of the Department of Homeland Security, 2006–2011.

Appendix 2
Legal Permanent Resident Flow by Region and Country of Birth: Fiscal Year 2011

REGION	NUMBER	PERCENT
Total	**1,062,040**	**100.0**
Africa	100,374	9.5
Asia	451,593	42.5
Europe	83,850	7.9
North America	333,902	31.4
Caribbean	133,680	12.6
Central America	43,707	4.1
Other North America	156,515	14.7
Oceania	4,980	0.5
South America	86,096	8.1
Unknown	1,245	0.1

(Continued)

COUNTRY OF BIRTH	NUMBER	PERCENT
Total	**1,062,040**	**100.0**
Mexico	143,446	13.5
China, People's Republic	87,016	8.2
India	69,013	6.5
Philippines	57,011	5.4
Dominican Republic	46,109	4.3
Cuba	36,452	3.4
Vietnam	34,157	3.2
Korea, South	22,824	2.1
Colombia	22,635	2.1
Haiti	22,111	2.1
Iraq	21,133	2.0
Jamaica	19,662	1.9
El Salvador	18,667	1.8
Bangladesh	16,707	1.6
Burma	16,518	1.6
Pakistan	15,546	1.5
Iran	14,822	1.4
Peru	14,064	1.3
Ethiopia	13,793	1.3
Canada	12,800	1.2
All other countries	357,554	33.7

SOURCE: US Department of Homeland Security. Computer Linked Applicant Information Management System (CLAIMS), Legal Immigrant Data. Fiscal Years 2009 to 2011.

Appendix 3
MPI Data Hub
Migration facts, Stats, and Maps

States Ranked by Number of Foreign Born: 1990, 2000, 2007, 2008, 2009, and 2010* (Table sorted by 2010 figures)

STATE	1990 ESTIMATE	1990 RANK	2000 ESTIMATE	2000 RANK	2007 ESTIMATE	2007 RANK	2008 ESTIMATE	2008 RANK	2009 ESTIMATE	2009 RANK	2010 ESTIMATE	2010 RANK
United States	19,767,316		31,107,889		38,059,694		37,960,935		38,517,234		39,955,854	
California	6,458,825	1	8,864,255	1	10,024,352	1	9,859,027	1	9,946,758	1	10,150,429	1
New York	2,851,861	2	3,868,133	2	4,205,813	2	4,236,768	2	4,178,170	2	4,297,612	2
Texas	1,524,436	4	2,899,642	3	3,828,904	3	3,887,224	3	3,985,239	3	4,142,031	3
Florida	1,662,601	3	2,670,828	4	3,440,918	4	3,391,511	4	3,484,141	4	3,658,043	4
New Jersey	966,610	5	1,476,327	6	1,731,202	6	1,718,034	6	1,759,467	5	1,844,581	5
Illinois	952,272	6	1,529,058	5	1,768,518	5	1,782,423	5	1,740,763	6	1,759,859	6
Massachusetts	573,733	7	772,983	7	913,957	8	937,200	7	943,335	7	983,564	7
Georgia	173,126	16	577,273	10	868,413	9	910,473	9	920,381	9	942,959	8
Virginia	311,809	12	570,279	11	794,246	11	795,712	11	805,742	11	911,119	9
Washington	322,144	10	614,457	9	795,179	10	804,364	10	810,637	10	886,262	10
Arizona	278,205	14	656,183	8	991,584	7	932,518	8	925,376	8	856,663	11
Maryland	313,494	11	518,315	13	694,590	12	697,609	12	730,400	12	803,695	12
Pennsylvania	369,316	8	508,291	14	665,176	13	660,426	13	691,242	13	739,068	13
North Carolina	115,077	21	430,000	15	629,947	14	641,130	14	665,270	14	719,137	14
Michigan	355,393	9	523,589	12	609,457	15	582,742	15	614,111	15	587,747	15
Nevada	104,828	23	316,593	19	497,821	17	490,717	17	506,505	16	508,458	16
Colorado	142,434	18	369,903	17	485,170	16	499,179	16	486,615	17	497,105	17
Connecticut	279,383	13	369,967	16	449,661	18	454,002	18	459,515	18	487,120	18
Ohio	259,673	15	339,279	18	419,443	19	427,040	19	433,330	19	469,748	19

Minnesota	113,039	22	260,463	21	345,001	21	340,657	21	357,561	21	378,483	20
Oregon	139,307	19	289,702	20	367,551	20	366,405	20	367,202	20	375,743	21
Indiana	94,263	25	186,534	24	263,848	22	256,125	22	281,327	22	300,789	22
Tennessee	59,114	31	159,004	25	249,552	24	248,483	23	265,658	23	288,993	23
Wisconsin	121,547	20	193,751	23	252,150	23	247,649	24	256,085	24	254,920	24
Hawaii	162,704	17	212,229	22	221,448	26	229,348	25	224,227	25	248,213	25
Missouri	83,633	27	151,196	27	208,121	28	215,214	27	212,900	27	232,537	26
Utah	58,600	33	158,664	26	215,757	25	226,440	26	218,142	26	222,638	27
South Carolina	49,964	34	115,978	32	190,014	29	195,069	28	205,133	28	218,494	28
Oklahoma	65,489	29	131,747	30	182,186	30	183,249	30	189,841	30	206,382	29
New Mexico	80,514	28	149,606	28	182,936	27	191,025	29	196,006	29	205,141	30
Kansas	62,840	30	134,735	29	167,085	31	164,118	31	171,252	31	186,942	31
Louisiana	87,407	26	115,885	33	143,267	34	134,704	32	152,002	32	172,866	32
Alabama	43,533	35	87,772	35	137,275	33	131,695	33	146,999	33	168,596	33
Kentucky	34,119	39	80,271	36	107,833	36	119,503	36	127,973	35	140,583	34
Iowa	43,316	36	91,085	34	117,437	35	112,289	35	116,161	37	139,477	35
Rhode Island	95,088	24	119,277	31	134,823	32	128,453	34	133,458	34	134,335	36
Arkansas	24,867	42	73,690	38	118,405	37	109,257	37	120,231	36	131,667	37
Nebraska	28,198	41	74,638	37	98,512	38	97,815	38	106,186	38	112,178	38
Idaho	28,905	40	64,080	40	83,904	39	89,489	39	97,642	39	87,098	39
District of Columbia	58,887	32	73,561	39	74,409	40	77,884	40	72,110	40	81,734	40
Delaware	22,275	44	44,898	42	65,821	42	66,793	41	74,033	41	71,858	41
New Hampshire	41,193	37	54,154	41	67,735	41	65,581	42	68,462	42	69,742	42
Mississippi	20,383	45	39,908	43	49,483	43	60,555	43	59,538	43	61,428	43
Alaska	24,814	43	37,170	44	48,928	44	44,296	44	48,849	44	49,319	44

(Continued)

(Continued)

STATE	1990		2000		2007		2008		2009		2010	
	ESTIMATE	RANK	ESTIMATE	RANK	ESTIMATE	RANK	ESTIMATE	RANK	ESTIMATE	RANK	ESTIMATE	RANK
Maine	36,296	38	36,691	45	44,464	45	39,378	45	43,958	45	45,666	45
Vermont	17,544	46	23,245	46	21,410	46	24,525	46	20,537	48	27,560	46
West Virginia	15,712	47	19,390	47	23,455	47	23,273	47	23,129	46	22,511	47
South Dakota	7,731	50	13,495	49	14,530	49	14,894	50	21,765	47	22,238	48
Montana	13,779	48	16,396	48	16,057	48	21,285	48	19,309	49	20,031	49
North Dakota	9,388	49	12,114	50	15,586	51	15,013	49	15,453	51	16,639	50
Wyoming	7,647	51	11,205	51	16,360	50	12,372	51	17,108	50	15,843	51

NOTES: *The term "foreign born" refers to people residing in the United States who were not US citizens at birth. The foreign-born population includes naturalized citizens, lawful permanent residents (LPRs), certain legal nonimmigrants (e.g., persons on student or work visas), those admitted under refugee or asylee status, and persons illegally residing in the United States. For information on sampling and nonsampling error, contact the US Census Bureau.

The noticeable increase in the number and share of the foreign born between 2009 and 2010 is partly attributed to changes in population weights between the two years (with ACS data prior to 2010 weighted to the 2000 Census, while the 2010 ACS is weighted to the 2010 Census). Higher response rates associated with the increased marketing and visibility surrounding the Decennial Census 2010 year likely also contributed to the shifts between the 2009 and 2010 ACS.

SOURCE: Table generated by Jeanne Batalova of the MPI Data Hub (Migration Policy Institute). Estimates for 1990 and 2000 are from the US Census Bureau, Summary File 3, 1990 and 2000 US Decennial Censuses; 2007, 2008, 2009, and 2010 estimates are from the US Census Bureau's American Community Surveys.

Suggested Reading

For a general account of immigration see Roger Daniels, *Coming to America* (2d ed.: New York: HarperCollins, 2002); Donna Gabaccia, *Immigration and American Diversity: A Social and Cultural History* (Malden, Mass.: Blackwell, 2002); Leonard Dinnerstein and David M. Reimers, *Ethnic Americans: A History of Immigration* (5th ed.; New York: Columbia University Press, 2009); Paul Spicard, *Almost All Aliens: Immigration, Race and Colonialism in American History and Identity* (New York: Routledge, 2007); and Mary C. Waters and Reed Ueda (eds.) with Helen B. Marrow, *The New Americans: A Guide to Immigration Since 1965* (Cambridge: Harvard University Press, 2007). Another general immigration history with much information on the post-1945 era is Susan A. Martin, *A Nation of Immigrants* (New York: Cambridge University Press, 2010). Information can also be found in Elliott Robert Barkan, *And Still They Come: Immigrants and American Society, 1920 to the 1990s* (Wheeling, Ill.: Harlan Davidson, 1996). The standard treatment of immigration law and policy is Aristide R. Zolberg, *A Nation by Design: Immigration Policy in the Fashioning of America* (Cambridge: Harvard University Press, 2006), but see Daniel Tichenor, *Dividing Lines: The Politics of Immigration Control in America* (Princeton: Princeton University Press, 2002). Two good books on contemporary immigration are Frank D. Bean and Gillian Stevens, *America's Newcomers and the Dynamics of Diversity* (New York: Russell Sage, 2003) and Richard Alba and Victor Nee, *Remaking the American Mainstream: Assimilation and Contemporary Immigration* (Cambridge: Harvard University Press, 2003). Also worth reading is Robert D. Putnam and David E. Campbell, *American Grace: How Religion Divides and Unites Us* (New York: Simon and Schuster, 2010). For immigrants in the suburbs, consult Audrey Singer, Susan W. Hardwick, and Caroline B. Brettel (eds.), *Twenty-First-Century Gateways: Immigrant Incorporation in Suburban America* (Washington: Brookings Institute Press, 2008).

General works on American history after 1945 are William H. Chafe, *The Unfinished Journey: America Since World War II* (6th ed.: New York: Oxford University Press, 2007) and Michael Schaller, Virginia Scharff, and Robert

Schulzinger, *Present Tense: The United States Since 1945* (3rd ed.: Boston: Cengage Learning, 2004).

A good introduction to European policies is Leo Lucassen, *The Immigrant Threat: The Integration of Old and New Migrants in Western Europe Since 1850* (Urbana: University of Illinois Press, 2005). See also Martin A. Schain, *The Politics of Immigration in France, Britain, and the United States* (New York: Palgrave Macmillan, 2008). A stunning book on Europe after 1945 is Tony Judt, *Postwar: A History of Europe Since 1945* (New York: The Penguin Press, 2005). For Canadian immigration policy, see Ninette Kelly and Michael Trelcock, *The Making of a Mosaic: A History of Canadian Immigration Policy* (2d ed.: Toronto: University of Toronto Press, 2010).

For the Irish see Linda Almeida, *Irish Immigrants in New York City, 1945–1995* (Bloomington: University of Indiana Press, 2001) and Mary P. Corcoran, *Illegal Irish* (Westport, CT: Greenwood Press, 1993). Other Europeans are covered in Annelise Orleck, *The Soviet Jewish Americans* (Westport, Conn.: Greenwood Press, 1999); Dennis Elliot Shasha and Marina Shron, *Red Blues: Voices from the Last Wave of Russian Immigrants* (New York: Holmes and Meier, 2002); and Carl J. Bon Tempo, *Americans at the Gate: The United States and Refugees During the Cold War* (Princeton: Princeton University Press, 2008). Another treatment of refugees, especially in the last thirty years, is David W. Haines, *Safe Haven: A History of Refugees in America* (Sterling, Va.: Kumarian Press, 2010). For displaced persons see Beth B. Cohen, *Case Closed: Holocaust Survivors in Postwar America* (New Brunswick, N.J.: Rutgers University Press, 2007). On the Poles see Helena Zaiecka Lopata, *Polish Americans* (New Brunswick, N.J.: Rutgers University Press, 1994). For the Jewish American response to the Holocaust, see Hasia Diner, *We Remember with Reverence: American Jews and the Myth of Silence After the Holocaust* (New York: New York University Press, 2010).

For Asian immigrants the literature has been growing. For Indians see Mitra S. Kalia, *Suburban Sahibs: Three Immigrant Families and the Passage to America* (New Brunswick: Rutgers University Press, 2003) and Madhulika S. Khandelwal, *Becoming American, Being Indian* (Ithaca: Cornell University Press, 2002). For Filipinos see Barbara Posada, *Filipino Americans* (Westport, Conn.: Greenwood Press, 1999). For refugees from Cambodia, consult Sucheng Chan, *Survivors: Cambodian Refugees in the United States* (Urbana: Illinois University Press, 2004); Min Zhou and Carl Bankston *Growing Up American: How Vietnamese Children Adapt to Life in the United States* (New York: Russell Sage, 1998); and Nancy D. Donnelly, *Changing Lives of Refugee Hmong Women* (Seattle: University of Washington Press, 1994).

Chinese women are treated in Xiaolan Bao, *Holding Up More Than Half the Sky: Chinese Garment Workers in New York City, 1948–1992* (Urbana: University of Illinois Press, 2001). For undocumented Chinese immigrants see Peter Kwong, *Forbidden Workers: Illegal Chinese Immigrants and American Labor* (New York: The New Press, 1997); Xiaojian Zhao, *The New Chinese America: Class, Economy, and Social Hierarchy* (New Brunswick, N.J.: Rutgers University Press, 2010); and

Patrick Radden Keefe, *The Snakehead: An Epic Tale of Chinatown Underworld and the American Dream* (New York: Doubleday, 2009). For other studies of Chinese immigrants, see Kenneth J. Guest, *God in Chinatown: Religion and Survival in New York's Evolving Immigrant Community* (New York: New York University Press, 2003); Min Zhou, *Contemporary Chinese America: Immigration, Ethnicity, and Community Transformation* (Philadelphia: Temple University Press, 2009); John Horton, *The Politics of Diversity: Immigration, Resistance, and Change in Monterey Park, California* (Philadelphia: Temple University Press, 1995); and Hiang-Shui Chen, *Chinatown No More: Taiwan Immigrants in Contemporary New York* (Ithaca: Cornell University Press, 1992).

For other Asians see John S. Park, *Elusive Citizenship: Immigration, Asian Americans, and the Paradox of Civil Rights* (New York: New York University Press, 2004) and Uma A. Segal, *A Framework for Immigration: Asians in the United States* (New York: Columbia University Press, 2002). For Koreans, see Ji-Yeon Yuh, *Beyond the Shadow of Camptown: Korean Military Brides in America* (New York: New York University Press, 2002); Susan Zeiger, *Entangling Alliances: Foreign War Brides and American Soldiers in the Twentieth Century* (New York: New York University Press, 2010); Nancy Abelmann and John Lie, *Blue Dreams: Korean Americans and the Los Angeles Riots* (Cambridge: Harvard University Press, 1995); and Pyong Gap Min, *Ethnic Solidarity for Economic Survival: Korean Green Greengrocers in New York City* (New York: Russell Sage, 2008).

For black immigrants consult Mary Waters, *Black Identities: West Indian Immigrant Dreams and American Realities* (Cambridge: Harvard University Press, 1999); Paul Stoller, *Money Has No Smell: The Africanization of New York City* (Chicago University of Chicago Press, 2000); and John A. Arthur, *Invisible Sojourners: African Immigrant Diaspora in the United States* (Westport, Conn.: Praeger, 2000).

The literature on the Middle East is only just beginning. The best place to begin is Anny Bakalian and Mehdi Bozorgmehr, *Backlash 9/11: Middle Eastern and Muslim Americans Respond* (Berkeley: University of California Press, 2009). See also Gregory Orfalea, *The Arab Americans: A History* (Northampton, Mass.: Olive Branch Press, 2005); and Shahnz Khan, *Muslim Women: Crafting a North American Identity* (Gainesville: University of Florida Press, 2000). An account of how Muslims are viewed in American society, especially through cartoons, see Peter Gottschalk and Gabriel Greenberg, *Islamophobia* (Lanham, Md.: Rowman and Littlefield Publishers, Inc., 2008).

There is a growing literature on Latinos. A general account is Roberto Suro, *Strangers Among Us: How Latino Immigration Is Transforming America* (New York: Alfred A. Knopf, 1998). A detailed statistical but controversial account is Laird W. Bergad and Herbert S. Klein, *Hispanics in the United States: A Demographic, Social, and Economic History, 1980–2005* (New York: Cambridge University Press, 2010). For New York City, consult Robert Smith, *Mexican New York: Transnational Lives of New Immigrants* (Berkeley: University of California Press, 2006) and Gabriel Thompson, *There's No Jose Here* (New York: Nation Books, 2007). See also Robert

Joe Stout, *Why Immigrants Come to America: Braceros, Indocumentados, and the Migra* (Westport, Conn.: Praeger, 2008). A new book on the Braceros is Deborah Colen, *Braceros: Migrant Citizens and Transnational Subjects in the Postwar United States and Mexico* (Chapel Hill: University of North Carolina Press, 2011).

Four other books on the border are worth reading: Jorge Ramos, *Dying to Cross: The Worst Immigrant Tragedy in American History* (New York: HarperCollins, 2005); Tim Gaynor, *Midnight on the Line: The Secret Life of the U.S.-Mexico Border* (New York: Thomas Dunne Books, 2009); Oscar J. Martinez, *Troublesome Border* (Tucson: University of Arizona Press, 2006); and Douglas Massey, Jorge Durand, and Noland J. Malone, *Beyond Smoke and Mirrors: Mexican Immigration in an Era of Economic Integration* (New York: Russell Sage, 2002). On politics and the border see David G. Gutierrez, *Walls and Mirrors: Mexican Americans, Mexican Immigration, and the Politics of Ethnicity* (Berkeley: University of California Press, 1991) and Armando Navarro, *The Immigration Crisis: Nativism, Armed Vigilantism, and the Rise of a Countervailing Movement* (Lanham, Md.: Rowman and Littlefield Publishers, Inc., 2009). Also useful is Peter Schrag, *Not Fit for Our Society: Nativism and Immigration* (Berkeley: University of California Press, 2010). For the issue of security, see Edward Alden, *The Closing of the American Border: Terrorism, Immigration and Security Since 9/11* (New York: HarperCollins, 2008).

For other information on Hispanics see Ruben Hernandez-Leon, *Metropolitan Migrants: The Migration of Urban Mexicans to the United States* (Berkeley: University of California Press, 2008). On the farmworkers movement see Randy Shaw, *Cesar Chavez, The UFW, and the Struggle for Justice in the 21st Century* (Berkeley: University of California Press, 2008). For Latinos in the South, see Gregory B. Weeks and John R. Weeks, *Irresistible Forces: Latin American Migration to the United States and Its Effects on the South* (Albuquerque: University of New Mexico Press, 2010).

For Cubans see Maria Cristina Garcia, *Havana USA: Cuban Exiles and Cuban Americans in South Florida, 1959-1994* (Berkeley: University of California Press, 1996) and Silvia Pedraza, *Political Disaffection in Cuba's Revolution and Exodus* (New York: Cambridge University Press, 2006). For other Latinos, see Leon Fink, *The Maya of Morgantown: Work and Community in the Nuevo New South* (Chapel Hill: University of North Carolina Press, 2003) and Cecilia Manjivar, *Fragmented Ties: Salvadoran Immigrant Networks in America* (Berkeley: University of California Press, 2000); Sarah J. Mahler, *American Dreaming: Immigrant Life on the Margins* (Princeton: Princeton University Press, 1995). For Brazilians see Maxine L. Margolis, *Little Brazil: An Ethnography of Brazilian Immigrants in New York City* (Princeton: Princeton University Press, 1994). See also David Badillo, *Latinos and the New Immigrant Church* (Baltimore: Johns Hopkins University Press, 2006); Alejandro Portes and Alex Stepick, *City on the Edge: The Transformation of Miami* (Berkeley: University of California Press, 1993); and Jennifer Gordon, *Suburban Sweatshops: The Struggle for Immigrant Rights* (Cambridge: Harvard University Press, 2005). Jesse Hoffnung-Garskof, *A Tale of Two Cities: Santo Domingo and New York After 1950* (Princeton: Princeton University Press, 2008) is especially good on Dominicans, but see also Sherri Grasmuck and Patricia R. Pessar, *Between Two Islands: Dominican International Migration* (Berkeley: University of California Press, 1991); and Jose Itzigsohn, *Encountering American Faultlines: Race, Class and the Dominican Experience in Providence* (New York: Russell Sage, 2009).

The Internet contains several sites for immigration. The Center for Immigration Studies (CIS.org) is a rich source, but its studies generally support lower levels of immigration. See also the Pew Hispanic Center (pewhispanic.org). The Department of Homeland Security has statistical material (DHS.gov) as does the American Community Survey of the Census (census.gov), while the reports of the Migration Information Source (migrationinformation.org) have many studies on recent immigration.

Index